100 Islamic Treasures

Principles from the Quran and the Sunnah for a better life

Samir Doudouch

© 2024 Muslimlife
Tous droits réservés.
ISBN: 978-1-952608-46-9
www.muslimlife.fr
contact@muslimlife.fr

Table of contents

Foreword 9

Chapter 1: Faith

1. Worshipping none but Allah 11
2. Following the Prophet Muhammad 13
3. Learning Islam 16
4. Reciting the Quran 18
5. Invoking Allah 20
6. Praying 22
7. Fasting 24
8. Repentance 25
9. Meditating on the Names & Attributes of Allah 27
10. Meditating on the Creation 29
11. Believing in the Prophets 31
12. Following the way of the Companions 33
13. Following the pious predecessors 36
14. Believing in the angels 40
15. Remembering death 44
16. Believing in the Day of Resurrection 46
17. Believing in Heaven 48
18. Believing in Hell 51
19. Avoiding major sins 53
20. Doing good deeds 55

Chapter 2: Health & Hygiene

21. Eating moderately 58

22. Eating and drinking with the right hand 60
23. Eating and drinking seated 62
24. Eating honey 64
25. Applying henna 65
26. Eating dates 66
27. Eating olive oil 67
28. Consuming black cumin 68
29. Sleeping like the Prophet 69
30. Not lying on your stomach 70
31. Practising a beneficial physical activity 71
32. Protecting yourself with Ayat al-Kursee 73
33. Healing yourself with surah Al-Fatiha 77
34. Protecting yourself with the last three surahs of
    the Quran 79
35. How to protect yourself with prophetic invocations 81
36. Practising Hijama 83
37. Using Siwak 84
38. Cutting your nails 85
39. Getting rid of some hair 86
40. Perfume 87

Chapter 3: Psychology

41. Having a good opinion of Allah 89
42. Crying 91
43. Observing the person below you 93
44. Show patience 95
45. Think of the consequences of our actions 96
46. Not worrying about the past 98
47. Not worrying about the future 99
48. Thinking before acting 100
49. Consulting Allah 101
50. Acting with constancy 102

51. Fighting laziness 103
52. Choosing the easy way 104
53. Fighting pride 105
54. Pushing back satanic insufflations 107
55. Fighting your soul 109
56. Channeling desires 111
57. Fighting envy 113
58. Controlling anger 114
59. Moderate laughter 116
60. Avoiding controversy 117

Chapter 4: Family & Relationships

61. Smile 119
62. Offering gifts 120
63. Visiting the sick 121
64. Reply to invitation 123
65. Hiding other people's faults 124
66. Giving advice 126
67. Responding to evil with good 127
68. No spying 128
69. Telling the truth 129
70. Behaving well with parents 131
71. Behaving well as husband and wife 135
72. Behaving well with children 137
73. Behaving well with neighbours 139
74. Minding our own business 141
75. Ask permission before entering 143
76. Lower your gaze 144
77. Avoid flattery 145
78. Avoid using foul language 147
79. Being grateful 149
80. Saluting others 150

Chapter 5: Finance

81. Getting up early 153
82. Working 154
83. Doing business 155
84. Getting married 157
85. Spending on good 159
86. Spending on students of religious science 160
87. Preserving family ties 161
88. Helping the weakest 162
89. Making the afterlife your main concern main 163
90. Alternate between Hajj and 'Umrah 164
91. Doing good 165
92. Hiding your plans 166
93. Only consume what is lawful 167
94. Keeping to the right path 168
95. Being grateful to Allah 169
96. Asking Allah for forgiveness 170
97. Fearing Allah 171
98. Applying what was revealed 172
99. Claiming protection against poverty 173
100. Trusting in Allah 174
Conclusion 175

بسم الله الرحمن الرحيم

Foreword

In the Name of Allah, the Most Gracious, the Most Merciful

This book aims to help Muslims improve their lives. That is why it lists 100 principles derived from the Quran and the Sunnah.

For better readability, these principles are classified into five categories that constitute the life of a Muslim:

1. **Faith**
2. **Health**
3. **Psychology**
4. **Relationships**
5. **Finances**

These principles are all drawn from Islam. Therefore, dear readers, you can be sure that implementing them will improve your life.

I ask Allah to make this modest work beneficial to its author and readers. Allah is sufficient for us, and He is the best Guardian.

Praise be to Allah, Lord of the Worlds, and may the blessings and peace of Allah be upon our Prophet Muhammad, his family, and his Companions.

Samir Doudouch

Chapter 1: Faith

1. Worshipping none but Allah

Allah said[1]:

"So, know that there is no god worthy of worship except Allah"[2]

"That is because Allah alone is the Truth, and what they invoke besides Him is falsehood, and Allah alone is truly the Most High, All-Great."[3]

"*Alif-Lâm-Râ*. This is a Book whose verses are well-perfected and then fully explained. It is from the One Who is All-Wise, All-Aware. Tell them, O Prophet: "Worship none but Allah. Surely I am a warner and deliverer of good news to you from Him.""[4]

"Surely, We sent Noah to his people. He said: "Indeed, I am sent to you with a clear warning that you should worship none but Allah. I truly fear for you the torment of a painful Day.""[5]

"And remember the brother of 'Âd, when he warned his people, who inhabited the sand-hills—there were certainly

---

[1] Translation of the meaning of the verses.
[2] Surah 47: Muhammad, verse 19.
[3] Surah 22: The Pilgrimage, verse 62.
[4] Surah 11: Hud, verses 1-2.
[5] Surah 11: Hud, verses 25-26.

warners before and after him—saying, "Worship none but Allah. I truly fear for you the torment of a tremendous day.""[1]

"Worship Allah and join none with Him in worship"[2]

"So worship Allah (Alone) by doing religious deeds sincerely for Allah's sake only."[3]

"Whoever disbelieves in *Taghut* and believes in Allah, then he has grasped the most trustworthy handhold that will never break. And Allah is All-Hearer, All-Knower."[4]

Remarks:

Monotheism is the most essential principle in Islam.

It is derived from the testimony of faith, the first pillar of Islam.

Indeed, the meaning of *"Lâ ilâha illa Allah"* is:

"There is no deity worthy of worship except Allah, and if other than Allah is worshipped, then that worship is in vain."

---

[1] Surah 46: The Dunes, verse 21.
[2] Surah 4: The Women, verse 36.
[3] Surah 39: The Groups, verse 2.
[4] Surah 2: The Cow, verse 256.

2. Following the Prophet Muhammad

Allah said:

"It is not for a believer, man or woman, when Allah and His Messenger have decreed a matter that they should have any option in their decision. And whoever disobeys Allah and His Messenger, he has indeed strayed in a plain error."[1]

"Only those are the believers who have believed in Allah and His Messenger, and afterwards doubt not but strive with their wealth and their lives for the Cause of Allah."[2]

"Say: "If you really love Allah, follow me; Allah will love you and forgive you of your sins. And Allah is Oft-Forgiving, Most Merciful. ""[3]

"Whatsoever the Messenger gives you, take it, and whatsoever he forbids you, abstain from it."[4]

---

[1] Surah 33: The Confederates, verse 36.
[2] Surah 49: The Dwellings, verse 15.
[3] Surah 3: Family of Imran, verse 31.
[4] Surah 59: The Exile, verse 7.

"O you who believe! Do not put yourselves forward before Allah and His Messenger, and fear Allah. Verily! Allah is All-Hearing, All-Knowing."[1]

"Verily, We have sent you (O Muhammad) as a witness, as a bearer of glad tidings, and as a warner so that you (O mankind) may believe in Allah and His Messenger and that you assist and honour him, and that you glorify Allah's praises morning and afternoon."[2]

The Prophet (peace and blessings of Allah upon him) said:

"None of you is a believer until I am dearer to him than his child, his father, and the whole of mankind."[3]

Remarks:

Following the Prophet (peace and blessings of Allah upon him) is a significant principle in Islam. It is derived from the testimony of faith, Islam's first pillar. Indeed, the meaning of "Muhammad Rasool Allah" is:

"No one is worthy of being followed besides the Messenger of Allah. Anyone followed without evidence besides the Messenger of Allah (peace and blessings of Allah upon him) is followed in vain."

"*Sunnah*" is a term that often comes up when discussing Islam. We also speak of Sunni Muslims. Therefore, it is

---

[1] Surah 49: The Dwellings, verse 1
[2] Surah 48: The Victory, verses 8-9
[3] Reported by Muslim.

vital to understand the scope and meaning of this word. The Sunnah encompasses what the Messenger of Allah (peace on him) was about concerning belief, words, deeds, and moderation. In a more straightforward and general way, the Sunnah is the tradition of the Prophet (peace and blessings of Allah upon him), his way of life. It explains the Quran. Indeed, we learn in the Quran that Muslims must pray, but through the Sunnah, we discover how we should pray (gestures, invocations, etc.).

The term "hadeeth" is also significant. It refers to the texts through which the Sunnah was communicated.

3. Learning Islam

Allah said:

"It is only those who have knowledge among His slaves that fear Allah."[1]

"And Allah has brought you out from the wombs of your mothers while you know nothing."[2]

"Allah bears witness that none has the right to be worshipped, but He, the angels, and those having knowledge also give this witness."[3]

"Allah will exalt in degree those of you who believe and those who have been granted knowledge."[4]

The Prophet (peace and blessings of Allah upon him) said:

"When a man dies, his acts come to an end but three: recurring charity, or knowledge (by which people) benefit, or a pious son who prays for him (for the deceased)."[5]

---

[1] Surah 35: The Originator, verse 28.
[2] Surah 16: The Bees, verse 78.
[3] Surah 3: Family of Imran, verse 18.
[4] Surah 58: The Woman Who Disputes, verse 11.
[5] Reported by Muslim.

The Prophet (peace and blessings of Allah upon him) said:

"If anyone travels on a road searching for knowledge, Allah will cause him to travel on one of the roads of Paradise. The angels will lower their wings in great pleasure with one who seeks knowledge; the inhabitants of the heavens and the Earth and the fish in the deep waters will ask forgiveness for the learned man. The superiority of the learned man over the devout is like that of the moon, on the night when it is full, over the rest of the stars. The learned are the heirs of the Prophets, and the Prophets leave neither dinar nor dirham, leaving only knowledge, and he who takes it takes an abundant portion."[1]

The Prophet (peace and blessings of Allah upon him) said:

"He to whom Allah intends to do good, He gives him insight into religion."[2]

Remarks:

Some scholars consider that the best thing a person can spend his life on is the study of Islam.

---

[1] Reported by Abu Dawud. Authenticated par Al-Albani.
[2] Reported by Muslim.

4. Reciting the Quran

The Prophet (peace and blessings of Allah upon him) said:

"Recite the Qur'an, for on the Day of Resurrection it will come as an intercessor for those who recite It."[1]

The Prophet (peace and blessings of Allah upon him) said:

"Such a person as recites the Qur'an and masters it by heart will be with the noble, righteous scribes (in Heaven). And such a person exerts himself to learn the Qur'an by heart and recites it with great difficulty will have a double reward."[2]

The Prophet (peace and blessings of Allah upon him) said:

"The example of him (a believer) who recites the Qur'an is like that of a citron which tastes good and smells good. And he (a believer) who does not recite the Qur'an is like a date which is good in taste but has no smell. The example of a dissolute, wicked person who recites the Qur'an is like the Raihana (sweet basil), which smells good but tastes bitter. And the example of a dissolute wicked person who does not

---

[1] Reported by Muslim.
[2] Reported by al-Bukhari.

recite the Qur'an is like the colocynth which tastes bitter and has no smell."[1]

The Prophet (peace and blessings of Allah upon him) said:

"Envy is not justified but in case of two persons only: one who, having been given (knowledge of) the Qur'an by Allah, recites it during the night and day and a man who, having been given wealth by God, spends it during the night and the day."[2]

Al-Bara' said:

"A man was reciting Surat Al-Kahf, and his horse was tied to two ropes beside him. A cloud came down and spread over that man, and it kept on coming closer and closer to him till his horse started jumping (as if afraid of something). When it was morning, the man went to the Prophet and told him of that experience. The Prophet (peace and blessings of Allah upon him) said: *"That was tranquillity which descended because of (the recitation of) the Qur'an."*"[3]

---

[1] Reported by al-Bukhari.
[2] Reported by Muslim.
[3] Reported by al-Bukhari.

5. Invoking Allah

Allah said:

"Then he invoked his Lord (saying): "I have been overcome, so help (me)!""[1]

"So invoke not with Allah another god lest you be among those who receive punishment."[2]

"And invoke not besides Allah, any that will neither profit nor hurt you."[3]

"Their way of request therein will be "Glory to You, O Allah!""[4]

The Prophet (peace and blessings of Allah upon him) said:

"No person suffers any anxiety or grief and says:

"O Allah, I am Your slave, son of Your slave, son of Your female slave, my forelock is in Your hand, Your Command over me is forever executed, and Your Decree over me is Just. I ask You by every Name belonging to You which You named Yourself with, or revealed in Your Book, or You taught to any

---

[1] Surah 54: The Moon, verse 10.
[2] Surah 26: The Poets, verse 213.
[3] Surah 10: Jonah, verse 106.
[4] Surah 10: Jonah, verse 10.

of Your Creation, or You have preserved in the knowledge of the unseen with You, that You make the Quran the life of my heart and the light of my breast, and a departure for my sorrow and a release for my anxiety."but Allah will take away his sorrow and grief and give him in their stead joy."[1]

Remarks:

Imam Ibn Al-Qayyim defines invocation as:"The imploration to realise what could be useful and the dissipation or removal of what is likely harmful."

---

[1] *Sahih Al-Kalim At-Tayyib* . Authenticated by al-Albani.

6. Praying

Allah said:

"When the prayers are over, remember Allah—whether you are standing, sitting, or lying down. But when you are secure, establish regular prayers. Verily, the prayer is enjoined on the believers at fixed hours."[1]

The Prophet (peace and blessings of Allah upon him) said:

"[..] Then the prayers were enjoined on me: fifty prayers daily. When I returned, I passed by Moses, who asked (me):"What have you been ordered to do?" I replied, "I have been ordered to offer fifty prayers daily." Moses said, "Your followers cannot bear fifty prayers a day, and by Allah, I have tested people before you, and I have tried my level best with Bani Israel (in vain). Return to your Lord and ask for reduction to lessen your followers' burden." So I went back, and Allah reduced ten prayers for me. Then again, I came to Moses, but he repeated the same as he had said before. Then again, I returned to Allah and He reduced ten more prayers. When I returned to Moses, he said the same: I went back to Allah, and He ordered me to observe ten prayers daily. When I returned to Moses, he repeated the same advice, so I returned

---

[1] Surah 4: The Women, verse 103.

to Allah and was ordered to observe five prayers daily. When I returned to Moses, he said, "What have you been ordered?" I replied, "I have been ordered to observe five prayers daily." He said, "Your followers cannot bear five prayers a day, and no doubt, I have got an experience of the people before you, and I have tried my level best with Bani Israel, so go back to your Lord and ask for reduction to lessen your follower's burden." I said, "I have requested so much of my Lord that I feel ashamed, but I am satisfied now and surrender to Allah's Order.""[1]

Remarks:

Prayer is the most important of the five pillars of Islam, directly after the attestation of faith. It includes several acts of worship, such as the remembrance of Allah, reciting the Quran, and prostration.

---

[1] Reported by al-Bukhari.

7. Fasting

Allah said:

"Eat and drink until the white thread (light) of dawn appears to you distinct from the black thread (darkness of night), then complete your fast till the nightfall."[1]

"The month of Ramadan in which was revealed the Quran, a guidance for humanity and clear proofs for the guidance and the criterion (between right and wrong). So, whoever is present this month, let them fast. But whoever is ill or on a journey, the same number from other days. Allah intends for you ease and does not want to make things difficult for you. (He wants that you) must complete the same number (of days), and that you must magnify Allah for having guided you so that you may be grateful to Him."[2]

The Prophet (peace and blessings of Allah upon him) said:

"Indeed, anyone who fasts for one day for Allah's Pleasure, Allah will keep his face away from the (Hell) fire for (a distance covered by a journey of) seventy years."[3]

---

[1] Surah 2: The Cow, verse 187.
[2] Surah 2: The Cow, verse 185.
[3] Reported by al-Bukhari.

8. Repentance

Allah said:

"Turn to Allah in repentance all together, O believers, so that you may be successful."[1]

"Seek the forgiveness of your Lord, and turn to Him in repentance, that He may grant you good enjoyment."[2]

"O you who believe! Turn to Allah with sincere repentance!"[3]

The Prophet (peace and blessings of Allah upon him) said:

"O people, seek repentance from Allah. Verily, I seek repentance from Him a hundred times a day."[4]

The Prophet (peace and blessings of Allah upon him) said:

"Allah is more pleased with the repentance of a servant as he turns towards Him for repentance than this that one amongst you is upon the camel in a waterless desert and there is upon (that camel) his provision of food and drink also, and

---

[1] Surah 24: The Light, verse 31.
[2] Surah 11: Hud, verse 3.
[3] Surah 66: The Prohibition, verse 8.
[4] Reported by Muslim.

he loses it, and he had lost all hope (to get that), lies down in the shadow and is disappointed about his camel, and there he finds that camel standing before him. He takes hold of his nose string and then, out of boundless joy, says: "O Lord, Thou art my servant, and I am Thine Lord." He commits this mistake out of extreme delight."[1]

Remarks: According to some scholars, repenting after sinning is obligatory. For repentance to be accepted, conditions must be met. If the sin concerns only the one who committed it and His Lord, he must:

- Renounce the sin in question
- Regret having sinned
- Make a firm decision never to do it again.

If the sin involves harming another person, a condition is added: compensation for the harm committed.

---

[1] Reported by Muslim.

9. Meditating on the Names & Attributes of Allah

Allah said:

"And the Most Beautiful Names belong to Allah, so call on Him by them, and leave the company of those who belie or deny His Names. They will be requited for what they used to do."[1]

"He is Allah, there is no god worthy of worship except Him the All-Knower of the unseen and the seen. He is the Most Beneficent, the Most Merciful. He is Allah; there is no god worthy of worship except Him, the King, the Holy, the One Free from all defects, the Giver of security, the Watcher over His creatures, the All-Mighty, the Compeller, the Supreme. Glory be to Allah! (High is He) above all that they associate as partners with Him. He is Allah, the Creator, the Inventor of all things, the Bestower of forms. To Him belong the Best Names. All that is in the heavens and the earth glorify Him. And He is the All-Mighty, the All-Wise."[2]

---

[1] Surah 7: The Heights, verse 180.
[2] Surah 59: The Exile, verses 22-24.

The Prophet (peace and blessings of Allah upon him) said:

"Allah has ninety-nine Names, one hundred less one; and he who memorised them all by heart will enter Paradise."[1]

Remarks:

Some scholars explain that it is necessary to learn Allah's names, understand them, and finally worship Him through them.

---

[1] Reported by al-Bukhari.

10. Meditating on the Creation

Allah said:

"Indeed, in the creation of the heavens and the earth and the alternation of the day and night, there are signs for people of reason, those who remember Allah while standing, sitting, and lying on their sides, and reflect on the creation of the heavens and the earth and pray: "Our Lord! You have not created this without purpose. Glory be to You! Protect us from the torment of the Fire.""[1]

"Or were they created by nothing, or are they creators? Or do they create the heavens and the earth? In fact, they have no certainty."[2]

Remarks:

Here are some examples of topics for meditation on the Creation:nature: its beauty, its diversity.

- the human being: its biological and psychological complexity.

- animals: their behaviours, their roles.

---

[1] Surah 3: The Family of Imran, verses 190-191.
[2] Surah 52: Mount Sinai, verses 35-36.

- celestial bodies: the stars, the planets, the sun, the moon.

11. Believing in the Prophets

Allah said:

"There are messengers whose stories We have told you already and others We have not. And to Moses Allah spoke directly."[1]

"And remember Our servants: Abraham, Isaac, Jacob— the men of strength and insight"[2]

"Messengers delivering good news and warnings so humanity should have no excuse before Allah after the coming of the messengers. And Allah is Almighty, All-Wise."[3]

"And when We took a covenant from the prophets, as well as from you, and Noah, Abraham, Moses, and Jesus, son of Mary. We did take a solemn covenant from them"[4]

"And We blessed David with Solomon—what an excellent servant! Indeed, he constantly turned to Allah."[5]

The Prophet (peace and blessings of Allah upon him) said:

---

[1] Surah 4: The Women, verse 164.
[2] Surah 38: Sad, verse 45.
[3] Surah 4: The Women, verse 165.
[4] Surah 33: The Clans, verse 7.
[5] Surah 38: Sad, verse 30.

"They will go to Noah and say; "O Noah! You are the first amongst the messengers of Allah to the people of the earth.""[1]

The Prophet (peace and blessings of Allah upon him) said:

"Moses said to Adam, "O Adam! You are our father who disappointed us and turned us out of Paradise!"

Then Adam said to him: "O Moses! Allah favoured you with His talk (talked to you directly), and He wrote (the Torah) for you with His Own Hand. Do you blame me for action which Allah had written in my fate forty years before my creation?"

So Adam confuted Moses, Adam confuted Moses".[2]

Remarks:

Islamic scholars consider a Prophet to be one who received the revelation but was not responsible for transmitting it.

As for a Messenger, he not only received the revelation but was also responsible for transmitting it.

From that place, they concluded that all messengers are prophets. However, not all prophets are necessarily messengers.

---

[1] Reported by al-Bukhari.
[2] Reported by al-Bukhari.

12. Following the way of the Companions

Allah said:

"Among the believers are men who have proven true to what they pledged to Allah. Some of them have fulfilled their pledge; others are waiting. They have never changed their commitment in the least."[1]

The Prophet (peace and blessings of Allah upon him) said:

"Do not abuse my Companions, for if any of you spent gold equal to Mount Uhud, it would not be equal to a Mud or even a half Mud spent by one of them."[2]

The Prophet (peace and blessings of Allah upon him) said:

"If I were to choose a bosom friend, I would have chosen Abu Bakr as my bosom friend, but he is my brother and my companion and Allah, the Exalted and Glorious, has taken

---

[1] Surah 33: The Clans, verse 23.
[2] Reported by al-Bukhari.

your brother and companion (meaning Prophet himself) as a friend."[1]

The Prophet (peace and blessings of Allah upon him) said:

"Among the nations before you, there used to be people who were inspired. And if there is any of such among my followers, it is 'Umar."[2]

The Prophet (peace and blessings of Allah upon him) was in 'Aisha's house. He had one of his thighs uncovered. Abu Bakr asked for permission to enter, and the Prophet (peace and blessings of Allah upon him) granted it. Then 'Umar knocked on the door and asked for permission to enter, and the Prophet (peace and blessings of Allah upon him) permitted him. Then Uthman knocked on the Prophet's door (peace and blessings of Allah upon him) and asked for permission to enter. The Prophet (peace and blessings of Allah upon him) covered his thigh and then permitted him. 'Aisha then asked the Prophet (peace and blessings of Allah upon him) why he did not cover his thigh when Abu Bakr and Umar entered but did so when Uthman entered.

The Prophet (peace and blessings of Allah upon him) answered:

---

[1] Reported by Muslim.
[2] Reported by al-Bukhari.

"Should I not feel shy before a man before whom the angels feel shy?"[1]

The Prophet (peace and blessings of Allah upon him) said about Ali Ibn Abu Talib:

"You are from me, and I am from you."[2]

Remarks:

The renowned scholar Ibn Rajab gave the following definition of the Companions: "Anyone who met the Prophet (peace and blessings of Allah upon him) and believed in his message and died as a Muslim."

---

[1] Reported by Muslim.
[2] Reported by al-Bukhari.

13. Following the pious predecessors

The Prophet (peace and blessings of Allah upon him) said:

"The best people are those of my generation, and then those who will come after them (the next generation), and then those who will come after them (i.e. the next generation)" [1]

Here are some words from the pious of the early generations:

Umar Ibn al Khattab (may Allah be pleased with him) said: "The one who laughs too much loses dignity. The one who jokes too much loses respect. Whoever does something a great deal becomes known for it. The one who speaks a great deal makes mistakes; the one who makes many mistakes loses his sense of dignity; whoever loses his sense of dignity loses his God-fearing, and whoever loses his God-fearing is spiritually dead. Do not speak what does not concern you, and move away from your enemy. The only trustworthy person fears Allah."

---

[1] Reported by al-Bukhari.

When Umar (may Allah be pleased with him) died, Medina darkened to such an extent that a child questioned his father in these terms, "Father, is it the day of the Resurrection?"

And he replied, "No, my son, but Umar was assassinated."

Ali Ibn Abu Talib (may Allah be pleased with him) said:

"The thing I fear most for you is following the desires and the hope of having a long life. Following our desires takes us away from the truth, and the hope of a long life makes us forget the afterlife."

"He who must die must really be humble."

"The thing of earthly life which the individual needs is food. So why does the individual worry in the morning, and does he work indescribably?"

"O you, know that you will soon go to people whose words will be silence."

Abdullah ibn Mas'oud (may Allah be pleased with him) said:

"Knowledge is not about having a lot of knowledge, but to know is to fear Allah."

"Woe to the uneducated, for if Allah had willed, He would have educated, and woe to him who does not put his knowledge into practice."(This phrase was repeated seven times)

"It behoves him who knows the Quran by heart to weep often, to be sad, wise, indulgent, and silent."

"By Allah, nothing deserves longer imprisonment than the tongue."

Mu'adh Ibn Jabal (may Allah be pleased with him) said: "O Allah, the eyes closed, the stars disappeared, and You, You are alive, and You exist by Yourself."

"You are going to experience misfortunes during which there will be a lot of money, and the Quran will be so open that all will read it, the believer and the hypocrite, the great and the small."

"When you pray, pray in the same way as the person who bids farewell, thinking you'll never come back."

When death came to him, he kept saying, "O Allah, I feared You, but today my hope is in You. You know I didn't like life on Earth and didn't want to stay there for long, but I liked being thirsty during heat waves, showing endurance for hours, and jostling scholars with my knees in study circles."

Salman al Farissi (may Allah be pleased with him) said:

"Knowledge is vast, life is short, so take the knowledge you need for your religion and leave the rest."

"If you sin in private, then commit a good action in private, and if you sin in public, then commit a good deed in public so that one erases the other."

Zayn al 'Abidine Ibn 'Ali ibn Al Husayn Ibn 'Ali ibn Abu Talib (may Allah be pleased with them) said: "In the past, the Quran was not sold, but the person would come with a sheet and stand next to the pulpit, and a volunteer would begin to write at the beginning of the sheet. Then another person would come and write the rest, and so on, until the Quran was completely written."

"I am amazed by the proud one, who yesterday was a drop of sperm, and tomorrow will be carrion."

Hassan Al Basri (may Allah have mercy on him) said: "The criticisms that the individual makes in public are, in fact, praise. If the individual hopes to live long, he will accomplish bad deeds. O human being, certainly, you are only a number; every day, a part of you is leaving. Your rulers are like your deeds, and you will be governed the same way you behave. Whoever competes with you in religion, compete with him, and he who competes with you for the goods of earthly life, throw them around his neck."

Sufyan at-Thawri said:

"Having many friends is a sign of weakness in religiosity."

He never sat at the head of an assembly, but he sat on the sides, close to the wall, and bent his legs. He said: "This is a time when you have to take care of yourself and when you have to leave other people."

14. Believing in the angels

Allah said:

"The angels are but honoured slaves. They speak not until He has spoken, and they act on His Command."[1]

"Those who are near Him (i.e. the angels) are not too proud to worship Him, nor are they weary (of His worship). They glorify His Praises night and day; they never slacken (to do so)."[2]

"And indeed, We have created man, and We know what his self whispers to him. And We are nearer to him than his jugular vein. Remember that the two recording angels receive, one sitting on the right and one on the left. Not a word does he utter, but a watcher by him is ready to record it."[3]

"And mention in the Book, the story of Mary, when she withdrew in seclusion from her family to a place facing east. She placed a screen from them; then We sent her Our Ruh[4], and he appeared before her in the form of a man in all respects. She said: "Verily! I seek refuge with the Most

---

[1] Surah 21: The Prophets, verses 26-27.
[2] Surah 21: The Prophets, verses 19-20.
[3] Surah 50: Qaf, verses 16-18.
[4] Angel Gabriel.

Beneficent (Allah) from you if you do fear Allah.". (The angel) said: "I am only a Messenger from your Lord, (to announce) to you the gift of a righteous son.""[1]

The Messenger of Allah (peace and blessings of Allah upon him) said :

"The Angels were born out of light, and the Jinns were born out of the spark of fire, and Adam was born as he has been defined for you."[2]

'Aisha said :

"The commencement of the Divine Inspiration to Allah's Messenger (peace and blessings of Allah upon him) was in the form of good dreams which came true like bright daylight, and then the love of seclusion was bestowed upon him. He used to go in seclusion in the cave of Hira, where he used to worship (Allah alone) continuously for many days before his desire to see his family. He used to take with him the journey food for the stay and then come back to (his wife) Khadija to take his food likewise again till suddenly the Truth descended upon him while he was in the cave of Hira. The angel came to him and asked him to read. The Prophet (peace and blessings of Allah upon him) replied, *"I do not know how to read."* The Prophet (peace and blessings of Allah upon him) added, *"The angel caught me (forcefully) and pressed me so hard that I could not bear it anymore. He then released me and asked me to read again,*

---

[1] Surah 19: Mary, verses 16-19.
[2] Reported by Muslim.

and I replied, 'I do not know how to read.' Thereupon, he caught me again and pressed me a second time till I could not bear it anymore. He then released me and asked me to read again, but I replied, 'I do not know how to read (or what shall I read)?' Thereupon, he caught me for the third time and pressed me, and then released me and said, 'Read in the name of your Lord, who has created (all that exists), created man from a clot. Read! And your Lord is the Most Generous.'"[1]

'Umar Ibn Al-Khattâb said :

One day, we were sitting in the company of Allah's Apostle (peace and blessings of Allah upon him) when a man dressed in pure white clothes and his hair extraordinarily black appeared before us. There were no signs of travel on him. None amongst us recognised him. At last, he sat with the Apostle (peace and blessings of Allah upon him). He knelt before him, placed his palms on his thighs and said: "Muhammad, inform me about Islam." The Messenger of Allah (peace and blessings of Allah upon him) said: *"Islam implies that you testify that there is no god who deserves worship but Allah and that Muhammad is the messenger of Allah, and you establish prayer, pay Zakat, observe the fast of Ramadan, and perform pilgrimage to the (House) if you are solvent enough (to bear the expense of) the journey"*. He (the inquirer) said: "You have told the truth." It amazed us that he would put the question and then verify the truth. He (the inquirer) said: "Inform me about faith." The Prophet

---

[1] Reported by al-Bukhari.

(peace and blessings of Allah upon him) replied: *"That you affirm your faith in Allah, in His angels, in His Books, in His Apostles, in the Day of Judgment, and in the Divine Decree about good and evil."* He (the inquirer) said: "You have told the truth." He (the inquirer) again said: "Inform me about *al-Ihsan* (performance of good deeds)." The Prophet (peace and blessings of Allah upon him) replied: *"That you worship Allah as if you are seeing Him, for though you don't see Him, He, verily, sees you."* He (the enquirer) again said: "Inform me about the hour (of the Doom)." The Prophet (peace and blessings of Allah upon him) replied: *"One who is asked knows no more than the one who is inquiring (about it)."* He (the inquirer) said: "Tell me some of its indications." The Prophet (peace and blessings of Allah upon him) replied: *"That the slave-girl will give birth to her mistress and master, that you will find barefooted, destitute goat herds vying with one another in the construction of magnificent buildings."* Then he (the inquirer) went on his way, but I stayed with him (the Prophet) for a long while. He then said to me: *"Umar, do you know who this inquirer was?"* I replied: "Allah and His Apostle know best." He (the Prophet) remarked: *"He was Gabriel (the angel). He came to you to instruct you in matters of religion."*[1]

---

[1] Reported by Muslim.

15. Remembering death

Allah said:

"Wherever you may be, death will overtake you even if you are in fortresses built up strong and high!"[1]

"Say (to them): "Verily, the death from which you flee will surely meet you, then you will be sent back to (Allah), the All-Knower of the unseen and the seen, and He will tell you what you used to do."[2]

"When their term is reached, they cannot delay or advance it by an hour (or a moment)."[3]

"(For) every matter there is a Decree (from Allah)"[4]

"Say: "The angel of death, who is set over you, will take your souls, then you shall be brought to your Lord.""[5]

The Prophet (peace and blessings of Allah upon him) said:

---

[1] Surah 4: The Women, verse 78.
[2] Surah 62: Friday, verse 8.
[3] Surah 10: Jonah, verse 49.
[4] Surah 13: The Thunder, verse 38.
[5] Surah 32: The Prostration, verse 11.

"Increase in remembrance of the severer of pleasures.» Meaning death.[1]

Remarks:

Scholars consider that remembering death contains several virtues, such as:

- The awakening of carefree hearts
- The revival of dead hearts
- The return of the servant to his Lord
- The softening of hearts
- Detachment from the life of this world

The events that follow death are :

- The settling in the grave
- The questioning by the two angels
- The arrival of the Day of Judgment
- The Scales
- The Crossing of the Bridge
- The entry into Paradise or Hell.

---

[1] Reported by al-Tirmidhi. Authenticated by al-Albani.

16. Believing in the Day of Resurrection

Allah said:

"And We shall set up balances of justice on the Day of Resurrection; then none will be dealt with unjustly in anything. And if there is a mustard seed's weight, We will bring it."[1]

"After that, indeed, you will die. Then (again), indeed, you will be resurrected on the Day of Resurrection."[2]

The Prophet (peace and blessings of Allah upon him) said:

"The people will be assembled on the Day of Resurrection barefooted, naked and uncircumcised".[3]

The Prophet (peace and blessings of Allah upon him) said:

"Allah will bring a believer near Him and shelter him with His Screen and ask him: Did you commit such-and-such sins? He will say: Yes, my Lord. Allah will keep on

---

[1] Surah 21: The Prophets, verse 47.
[2] Surah 23: The Believers, verses 15-16.
[3] Reported by al-Bukhari & Muslim.

asking him till he confesses all his sins and will think that he is ruined. Allah will say: 'I did screen your sins in the world, and I forgive them for you today', and then he will be given the book of his good deeds. Regarding infidels and hypocrites (their evil acts will be exposed publicly), the witnesses will say: These are the people who lied against their Lord. Behold! The Curse of Allah is upon the wrongdoers."[1]

---

[1] Reported by al-Bukhari & Muslim.

17. Believing in Heaven

Allah said:

"And those foremost [in the life of this world on the very first call for to embrace Islam] will be foremost (in Paradise). These will be those nearest to Allah, in the Gardens of delight. Many of those (foremost) will be from the first generations (who embraced Islam). And a few of those will be from the later time (generations). (They will be) on thrones woven with gold and precious stones, Reclining thereon, face to face. Immortal boys will serve them with cups, jugs, and a glass of the flowing wine, where they will get neither aching of the head nor intoxicated. And fruit; that they may choose. And the flesh of fowls that they desire. And (there will be) Houris (fair females) with wide, lovely eyes, like unto preserved pearls. A reward for what they used to do. They will hear no evil, vain talk, or any sinful speech. But only the saying of "Salam! Salam!" (greetings with peace)! And those on the Right Hand – Who will be those on the Right Hand? (They will be) among thornless lote-trees, among banana trees with fruits piled one above another, in the shade long-extended, by water flowing constantly, and fruit in plenty, whose season is not limited, and their supply will not be cut off, and on couches or thrones, raised high. Verily, We have created them (maidens) of special creation. And made them virgins. Loving (their husbands only), equal in age."[1]

"But those who fear Allah and keep their duty to their Lord (Allah), for them are built lofty rooms; one above another under which rivers flow. (This is) the Promise of Allah: and Allah does not fail in (His) Promise."[2]

The Prophet (peace and blessings of Allah upon him) said:

"Gabriel then travelled with me until we reached the farthest lote tree. Many colours had covered it, which I do not know. Then I was admitted to Paradise and saw in it domes of pearls and its soil of musk."[3]

The Prophet (peace and blessings of Allah upon him) said:

"When (Allah's) slave is put in his grave, and his companions return, and he even hears their footsteps, two angels come to him and make him sit and ask, 'What did you use to say about this man (i.e. Muhammad)?' The faithful Believer will say, 'I testify that he is Allah's slave and His Apostle.' Then they will say to him, 'Look at your place in the Hell Fire; Allah has given you a place in Paradise instead of it.'"

---

[1] Surah 56: The Event, verses 10-37.
[2] Surah 39: The Groups, verse 20.
[3] Reported by al-Bukhari & Muslim.

Allah's Messenger (peace and blessings of Allah upon him) said: *"He would be shown both the seats."*[1]

The Prophet (peace and blessings of Allah upon him) said:

"Paradise became so near to me that if I had dared, I would have plucked one of its bunches for you, and Hell became so near to me that I said: 'O my Lord, will I be among those people?'"[2]

---

[1] Reported by al-Bukhari & Muslim.
[2] Reported by al-Bukhari.

18. Believing in Hell

Allah said:

"Verily, the hypocrites will be in the lowest depths of the Fire"[1]

"Is then one who seeks the good Pleasure of Allah like the one who draws on himself the Wrath of Allah? – his abode is Hell – and worst, indeed, is that destination!"[2]

"The Fire will burn their faces, and therein they will grin, with displaced lips."[3]

Ibn 'Umar — may Allah be pleased with him — said :

"There came to me (in a dream) two angels. In the hand of each of them, there was a mace of iron [...] Then I saw myself being confronted by another angel holding a mace of iron in his hand. He said to me: "Do not be afraid; you will be an excellent man if you only pray more often."

So they took me until they stopped me at the edge of Hell, and behold, it was built inside like a well, and it had side posts like those of a well. Besides each post, an angel was carrying an iron mace. I saw therein many people hanging

---

[1] Surah 4: The Women, verse 145.
[2] Surah 3: Family of Imran, verse 162.
[3] Surah 23: The Believers, verse 104.

upside down with iron chains, and I recognised therein some men from the Quraish. Then (the angels) took me to the right side. I narrated this dream to (my sister) Hafsa, and she told it to Allah's Messenger (peace and blessings of Allah upon him). Allah's Messenger (peace and blessings of Allah upon him) said: *"No doubt, Abdullah is a good man."*[1]

The Prophet (peace and blessings of Allah upon him) said:

"The width between the two shoulders of a disbeliever will be equal to the distance covered by a fast rider in three days."[2]

---

[1] Reported by al-Bukhari & Muslim.
[2] Reported by al-Bukhari & Muslim.

19. Avoiding major sins

Allah said:

"If you avoid the great sins which you are forbidden to do, We shall remit your (small) sins from you and admit you to a Noble Entrance."[1]

"Verily, Allah forgives not that partners should be set up with him in worship, but He forgives except that (anything else) to whom He pleases, and whoever sets up partners with Allah in worship has indeed invented a tremendous sin."[2]

The Prophet (peace and blessings of Allah upon him) said:

"Avoid the seven great destructive sins."

They (the people!) asked, "O Allah's Apostle! What are they?" He said: *"To join partners in worship with Allah; to practice sorcery; to kill the life which Allah has forbidden except for a just cause (according to Islamic law); to eat up usury, to eat up the property of an orphan; to give one's back to the enemy and fleeing from the battle-field at the time of*

---

[1] Surah 4: The Women, verse 31.
[2] Surah 4: The Women, verse 48.

fighting and to accuse chaste women who never even think of anything touching chastity and are good believers."[1]

The Prophet (peace and blessings of Allah upon him) said:

"Shall I not inform you of the greatest of the major sins? To join partners in worship with Allah, disobeying parents, and false testimony."[2]

---

[1] Reported by al-Bukhari & Muslim.
[2] Reported by al-Bukhari & Muslim.

20. Doing good deeds

Allah said:

"Say (O Muhammad): "I am only a man like you. I have been inspired that your God) is One. So whoever hopes for the Meeting with his Lord, let him work righteousness and associate none as a partner in the worship of his Lord."[1]

"Wealth and children are the adornment of the life of this world. But the good, righteous deeds, that last, are better with your Lord for rewards and better in respect of hope."[2]

"Those who believe and do righteous good deeds, surely, We shall remit from them their evil deeds and shall reward them according to the best of what they used to do."[3]

"By the Time. Verily! Man is in loss, except those who believe and do righteous good deeds, recommend one another to the truth, and recommend one another to patience."[4]

Abu Dhar, may Allah be pleased with him, reported:

---

[1] Surah 18: The Cave, verse 110.
[2] Surah 18: The Cave, verse 46.
[3] Surah 29: The Spider, verse 7.
[4] Surah 103: The Time, verses 1 to 3.

"O Messenger of Allah, advise me".

The Prophet (peace and blessings of Allah upon him) said:

"If you do a bad deed, follow it with a good deed to erase it."

I said: "O Messenger of Allah, is *"La Ilaha Illa Allah"* among the good deeds ?"

The Prophet (peace and blessings of Allah upon him) replied: *"It is the best of all good deeds."*[1]

---

[1] Reported by Ahmad. Authenticated by al-Albani.

Chapter 2: Health & Hygiene

21. Eating moderately

The Prophet (peace and blessings of Allah upon him) said:

"The human does not fill any container worse than his stomach. It is sufficient for the son of Adam to eat what will support his back. If this is not possible, then a third for food, a third for drink, and a third for his breath."[1]

It is reported that Imam Al-Shafi'i said:

"For sixteen years, I have not been fully satiated, except once when I vomited because satiety weighs down the body, hardens the heart, diminishes discernment, induces sleep and weakens one in performing acts of worship."

Remarks:

According to Imam Ibn Al-Qayyim, there are 3 degrees of nutrition: the degree of need, the degree of sufficiency and the degree of excess.

He goes on to explain that if we do not follow the recommendations in the hadeeth, we risk exposing our bodies to fatigue and other ailments.

---

[1] Reported by al-Tirmidhi. Authenticated by al-Albani.

Among these evils, he cites corruption of the heart, laziness, and inclinations towards desires. He then deduced that overeating harms both the heart and the body.

However, Imam Ibn Al-Qayyim points out that the harmful effects manifest when we eat frequently in excess. On the other hand, if this only happens occasionally, there is no harm.

To illustrate his point, Imam Ibn Al-Qayyim reports that the Companions ate to satiety several times in the presence of the Prophet (peace and blessings of Allah upon him).

22. Eating and drinking with the right hand

The Prophet (peace and blessings of Allah upon him) said:

"When any of you intends to eat (meal), he should eat with his right hand and when he (intends) to drink, he should drink with his right hand, for Satan eats with his left hand and drinks with his left hand."[1]

'Umar ibn Abi Salama — may Allah be pleased with him — reported:

"I was a boy under the care of Allah's Messenger (peace and blessings of Allah upon him), and my hand used to go around the dish while I was eating. So Allah's Messenger (peace and blessings of Allah upon him) said to me: 'O boy! Mention the Name of Allah, eat with your right hand, and eat of the dish what is nearer to you.'"[2]

Salama ibn Al-Akwa' — may Allah be pleased with him — reported that a person ate in the presence of Allah's Messenger (peace and blessings of Allah upon him) with his left hand, after that he said:

---
[1] Reported by Muslim.
[2] Reported by al-Bukhari & Muslim.

"Eat with your right hand."

He said: "I cannot do that", whereupon he (the Holy Prophet) said: *"May you not be able to do that."*

The narrator added:

"It was vanity that prevented him from doing it, and he could not raise it (the right hand) up to his mouth."[1]

Remarks:

Scholar Al-'Uthaymeen explains these two texts and concludes that eating and drinking with the right hand is obligatory. He adds that eating and drinking with the left hand is prohibited and that anyone who does so has committed a sin. He also informs us that eating and drinking with the left hand is a form of imitation of the devil and his followers. However, he notes that if a person has a good reason (such as paralysis of the right hand), there is no harm in using the left hand.

---

[1] Reported by Muslim.

23. Eating and drinking seated

Anas reported that Allah's Apostle (peace and blessings of Allah upon him) forbade that a person should drink while standing. Qatada reported:

We said to him: "What about eating?" He (Anas) said, "That is even worse and more detestable."[1]

The Prophet (peace and blessings of Allah upon him) said:

"None of you should drink while standing, and if anyone forgets, he must vomit."[2]

Remarks:

In his commentary on these ahadeeth, the scholar Al-'Utheymeen explains that it is preferable to eat and drink sitting down, as the Prophet (peace and blessings of Allah upon him) recommended.

However, he explains that it is permissible to do so standing up, as there is proof of this effect:

---

[1] Reported by Muslim.
[2] Reported by Muslim.

Ibn 'Abbas reported:

"I served (water of) Zamzam to Allah's Messenger (peace and blessings of Allah upon him), and he drank it while standing."[1]

Al-Nazzal Ibn Sabra reported:

"'Ali came to the gate of the courtyard and drank while he was standing and said: "Some people dislike drinking while standing, but I saw the Prophet (peace and blessings of Allah upon him) doing (drinking water) as you have seen me doing now.""[2]

The shaykh concludes by explaining that although eating and drinking while standing is permissible, it is preferable to do so while seated.

---

[1] Reported by al-Bukhari & Muslim.
[2] Reported by al-Bukhari.

24. Eating honey

Allah said:

"And your Lord inspired the bee, saying: "Take you habitations in the mountains, the trees, and what they erect. Then, eat of all fruits, and follow the ways of your Lord made easy (for you)." There comes forth from their bellies a drink of varying colours that is healing for men. Verily, in this is indeed a sign for people who think."[1]

The Prophet (peace and blessings of Allah upon him) said:

"Healing is in three things: cupping, a gulp of honey or cauterisation (branding with fire), but I forbid my followers to use cauterisation."[2]

---

[1] Surah 16: The Bees, verses 68-69.
[2] Reported by al-Bukhari.

25. Applying henna

Salma Umm Rafi', the freed slave woman of the Messenger of Allah (peace and blessings of Allah upon him), said:

"The Prophet (peace and blessings of Allah upon him) did not suffer any injury or thorn-prick, but he would apply henna to it."[1]

Remarks:

Imam Nawawi said: "It is forbidden for a man to put henna on his hands or feet, except for self-care."

---

[1] Reported by Ibn Majah. Authenticated by al-Albani.

26. Eating dates

Allah said:

"And shake the date palm trunk towards you; it will let fresh ripe dates fall upon you. So eat and drink and be glad."[1]

The Prophet (peace and blessings of Allah upon him) said:

"Whoever takes seven 'Ajwa dates in the morning will not be affected by magic or poison on that day."[2]

The Prophet (peace and blessings of Allah upon him) said:

"Al-'Ajwah is from Paradise, and it contains a cure for poison."[3]

Abu Musa reported :"A child was born in my house. I brought him to Allah's Apostle (may peace be upon him). He gave him the name Ibrahim, and he rubbed his palate with dates."[4]

---

[1] Surah 19: Mary, verses 25-26.
[2] Reported by al-Bukhari & Muslim.
[3] Reported by al-Tirmidhi. Authenticated by al-Albani.
[4] Reported by al-Bukhari & Muslim.

27. Eating olive oil

Allah said:

"And a tree (olive) that springs forth from Mount Sinai, that grows oil, and (it is a) relish for the eaters."[1]

"Allah is the Light of the heavens and the earth. The parable of His Light is as (if there were) a niche and within it a lamp; the lamp is in glass, the glass as it were a brilliant star, lit from a blessed tree, an olive, neither of the east nor the west, whose oil would almost glow forth (of itself), though no fire touched it. Light upon Light! Allah guides to His Light whom He wills. And Allah sets forth parables for humanity, and Allah is All-Knower of everything."[2]

The Prophet (peace and blessings of Allah upon him) said:

"Eat of its oil and use it (the olives), for indeed it is from a blessed tree."[3]

---

[1] Surah 23: The Believers, verse 20.
[2] Surah 24: The Light, verse 35.
[3] Reported by al-Tirmidhi. Authenticated by al-Albani.

28. Consuming black cumin

'Aisha has narrated that she heard the Prophet (peace and blessings of Allah upon him) saying: *'This black cumin is healing for all diseases except As-Sam.'* Aisha said, 'What is As-Sam?' He said, *'Death'.*"[1]

The Prophet (peace and blessings of Allah upon him) said:

"There is healing in black cumin for all diseases except death."[2]

---

[1] Reported by al-Bukhari.
[2] Reported by al-Bukhari.

29. Sleeping like the Prophet

Abu Barza al-Aslami reported:

"The Prophet (peace and blessings of Allah upon him) preferred to pray the 'Isha' late and disliked sleeping before or talking after it."[1]

Al-Bara Ibn 'Azib reported: "The Messenger of Allah (peace and blessings of Allah upon him) said to me: *"When you want to go to bed, perform ablution as you do for prayer"*[2]

The Messenger of Allah (peace and blessings of Allah upon him) said:

"When any of you goes to bed, he should dust it off thrice with the edge of his garment and say: "In Your Name, Lord, I have laid down my side, and in Your Name I raise it. If You take my soul, be merciful to it, and if You resurrect it, protect it with the means You use to protect Your virtuous servants.""[3]

Al-Bara Ibn 'Azib reported: "The Messenger of Allah (peace and blessings of Allah upon him) said to me : *"Then lie down on your right side."*[4]

---

[1] Reported by al-Bukhari & Muslim.
[2] Reported by al-Bukhari & Muslim.
[3] Reported by al-Bukhari & Muslim.
[4] Reported by al-Bukhari & Muslim.

30. Not lying on your stomach

Teekhfah Ibn Qays al-Gheefari reported that his father said:

"I was a guest of the Messenger of Allah (peace be upon him) among other poor guests. The Messenger of Allah (peace be upon him) came out at night to check on his guests and saw me lying on my stomach. He nudged me with his foot and said: *"Do not lie down in this manner; this is a way of lying down that Allah dislikes."*"

In another version: "He nudged me with his foot and said:

"This is how the people of Hell lie.""[1]

Remarks:

The scholar Al-'Uthaymeen specifies that in the event of pain, if sleeping on the stomach relieves it, then there is no harm in it.

---

[1] Reported by Abu Dawud. Authenticated by al-Albani.

31. Practising a beneficial physical activity

The Prophet (peace and blessings of Allah upon him) said:

"A strong believer is better and dearer to Allah than a weak one, and both are good."[1]

The Prophet (peace and blessings of Allah upon him) said:

"Everything that does not involve the remembrance of Allah, the Almighty, is frivolity or oversight, except for four things: walking between two targets[2], training his horse, playing with his wife and teaching swimming".[3]

'Aisha — may Allah be pleased with her — reported:

"I went out with the Prophet (peace be upon him) on one of his journeys when I was a young girl, slim and trim. He said to the people: *"Go ahead,"* and they went ahead. Then he said to me: *"Come on, let's race."*

---

[1] Reported by Muslim.
[2] This means archery training.
[3] Authenticated by al-Albani.

I raced him and outpaced him. He did not mention it again until I had grown heavier and had forgotten about it. We went out again on one of his journeys, and he said to the people: *"Go ahead,"* and they did. Then he said, *"Come on, let's race."*

I raced him, and this time he outpaced me. He laughed and said, *"This one for that one."*[1]

---

[1] Reported by al-Nassai. Authenticated by al-Albani.

32. Protecting yourself with Ayat al-Kursee

The verse is as follows:

"Allah! *La ilaha illa Huwa* (none has the right to be worshipped but He), the Ever Living, the One Who sustains and protects all that exists. Neither slumber nor sleep overtakes Him. To Him belongs whatever is in the heavens and whatever is on earth. Who is he that can intercede with Him except with His Permission? He knows what happens to them (His creatures) in this world and what will happen to them in the Hereafter. And they will never compass anything of His Knowledge except that He wills. His Kursi extends over the heavens and the earth, and He feels no fatigue in guarding and preserving them. And He is the Most High, the Most Great."[1]

Abu Hurayra — may Allah be pleased with him — reported:

"Allah's Messenger (peace be upon him) deputed me to keep Zakat (al-Fitr) of Ramadan. A comer came and started taking handfuls of the foodstuff (of the Sadaqa)

---
[1] Surah 2: The Cow, verse 255.

(stealthily). I took hold of him and said, "By Allah, I will take you to Allah's Messenger (peace be upon him)."

He said, "I am needy, have many dependents, and am in great need". I released him, and in the morning, Allah's Messenger (peace be upon him) asked me, *"What did your prisoner do yesterday?"*

I said, "O Allah's Messenger (peace be upon him)! The person complained of being needy and having many dependents, so I pitied him and let him go."

Allah's Messenger (peace be upon him) said, *"Indeed, he told you a lie, and he will be coming again."*

I believed that he would reappear as Allah's Messenger (peace be upon him) had told me he would return. So, I waited for him watchfully. When he (showed up and) started stealing handfuls of foodstuffs, I caught hold of him again and said, "I will definitely take you to Allah's Messenger (peace be upon him). He said, "Leave me, for I am very needy and have many dependents. I promise I will not come back again." I pitied him and let him go. In the morning, Allah's Messenger (peace be upon him) asked me, *"What did your prisoner do?"*

I replied, "O Allah's Messenger (peace be upon him)! He complained of his great need and of too many dependents, so I took pity on him and set him free."

Allah's Apostle said, *"Verily, he told you a lie, and he will return."*

I waited for him attentively for the third time, and when he (came and) started stealing handfuls of the foodstuff, I caught hold of him and said, "I will surely take you to Allah's Messenger (peace be upon him) as it is the third time you promise not to return, yet you break your promise and come."

He said, "(Forgive me and) I will teach you some words with which Allah will benefit you."

I asked, "What are they?" He replied, "Whenever you go to bed, recite "Ayat-al-Kursi"- 'Allahu la ilaha illa huwa-l-Haiy-ul Qaiyum'—until you finish the whole verse. (If you do so), Allah will appoint a guard for you who will stay with you, and no Satan will come near you until morning. "So, I released him. In the morning, Allah's Apostle asked, *"What did your prisoner do yesterday?"*

I replied, "He claimed that he would teach me some words by which Allah would benefit me, so I let him go."

Allah's Messenger (peace be upon him) asked, *"What are they?"* I replied, "He said to me, 'Whenever you go to bed, recite Ayat-al-Kursi from the beginning to the end ---- Allahu la ilaha illa huwa-lHaiy-ul-Qaiyum----.'

He further said to me, '(If you do so), Allah will appoint a guard who will stay with you, and no Satan will come near you until morning.'

The Prophet (peace be upon him) said, *"He spoke the truth, although he is an absolute liar. Do you know whom you were talking to, these three nights, O Abu Huraira?"* I said, "No." He said, *"It was Satan."*[1]

---
[1] Reported by al-Bukhari.

33. Healing yourself with surah Al-Fatiha

Surah *Al-Fatiha* is as follows:

"All the praises and thanks be to Allah, the Lord of the 'Alamin (humankind, jinns and all that exists). The Most Beneficent, the Most Merciful. The Only Owner of the Day of Recompense. You (Alone) we worship, and You we ask for help. Guide us to the Straight Way. The Way of those on whom You have bestowed Your Grace, not of those who earned Your Anger, nor of those who went astray."[1]

"A group of the companions of Allah's Messenger (peace be upon him) proceeded on a journey till they dismounted near one of the Arab tribes and requested them to entertain them as their guests, but they (the tribe people) refused to entertain them. Then, the tribe chief was bitten by a snake (or stung by a scorpion), and he was given all sorts of treatment, but all were in vain. Some said, "Will you go to the group (those travellers) who have dismounted near you and see if one of them has something useful?"

---

[1] Surah 1: The Opener.

They came to them and said, "O the group! Our leader has been bitten by a snake (or stung by a scorpion), and we have treated him with everything, but nothing benefited him. Has anyone of you anything useful?"

One replied, "Yes, by Allah, I know how to treat with a *Ruqya*. But, by Allah, we wanted you to receive us as your guests, but you refused. I will not treat your patient with a Ruqya until you fix something for us as wages."

Consequently, they agreed to give those travellers a flock of sheep. The man went with them (the tribe's people) and started spitting (on the bite) and reciting *Surat-al-Fatiha* till the patient was healed and started walking as if he had not been sick. When the tribe people paid them the wages they had agreed upon, some of them (the Prophet's companions) said, "Distribute (the sheep)."

But the one who treated with the *Ruqya* said, "Do not do that till we go to Allah's Apostle and mention to him what has happened and see what he will order us."

So they came to Allah's Messenger (peace be upon him) and mentioned the story to him, and he said, *"How do you know that Surat-al-Fatiha is a Ruqya? You have done the right thing. Divide (what you have got) and assign for me a share with you."*[1]

---

[1] Reported by al-Bukhari & Muslim.

34. Protecting yourself with the last three surahs of the Quran

The last three surahs of the Quran are the following:

"Say: 'He is Allah, (the) One. *Allah-us-Samad* (The Self-Sufficient Master). He begets not, nor was He begotten, and there is none co-equal or comparable unto Him.'"[1]

"Say: 'I seek refuge with the Lord of the daybreak, from the evil of what He has created; and from the evil of the darkening (night) as it comes with its darkness. And from the evil of the witchcrafts when they blow in the knots, and from the evil of the envier when he envies.'"[2]

"Say: 'I seek refuge with the Lord of mankind, the King of mankind, the *Ilah* (God) of mankind, from the evil of the whisperer (devil who whispers evil in the hearts of men) who withdraws, who whispers in the breasts of mankind, of jinns and men.'"[3]

---

[1] Surah 112: The Sincerity.
[2] Surah 113: The Daybreak.
[3] Surah 114: The Mankind.

'Aisha — may Allah be pleased with her — reported: "Whenever the Prophet (peace and blessings of Allah upon him) went to bed every night, he used to cup his hands together and blow over it after reciting *Surat Al-Ikhlas, Surat Al-Falaq* and *Surat An-Nas*, and then rub his hands over whatever parts of his body he was able to rub, starting with his head, face and front of his body. He used to do that three times."[1]

'Aisha — may Allah be pleased with her — reported: "When Allah's Messenger (peace and blessings of Allah upon him) fell ill, he recited over his body *Mu'awwidhatan* and blew over him, and when his sickness was aggravated, I used to recite over him and rub him with his band with the hope that it was more blessed."[2]

---

[1] Reported by al-Bukhari.
[2] Reported by al-Bukhari.

35. How to protect yourself with prophetic invocations

The Prophet (peace and blessings of Allah upon him) said:

"When anyone lands at a place and then says:

"I seek refuge in the Perfect Word of Allah from the evil of what He has created," nothing would harm him until he marches from that stopping place."[1]

'Uthman Ibn Abi Al-'As reported that he made a complaint of pain to Allah's Messenger (peace and blessings of Allah upon him) that he felt in his body at the time he had become Muslim. Thereupon Allah's Messenger (peace and blessings of Allah upon him) said:

"Place your hand at the place where you feel pain in your body and say "Bismillah" (in the name of Allah) three times and "I seek refuge with Allah and with His Power from the evil that I find and that I fear." seven times."[2]

When Allah's Messenger (peace and blessings of Allah upon him) visited a sick of his family, he said: *'Lord of the*

---

[1] Reported by Muslim.
[2] Reported by Muslim.

people. remove the disease, cure him, for Thou art the great Curer, there is no cure but through Thine healing Power, which leaves nothing of the disease'."[1]

Remarks:

Imam Ibn Al-Qayyim explains:"Whoever tries these invocations and searches for protection will see their usefulness and necessity. They prevent the evil eye from having its effect. If it does, they repel it according to the faith of the one who utters them, the strength of his soul, his disposition, his trust in Allah and the firmness of his heart. They are a weapon, and the weapon depends on the one who carries it ".

---

[1] Reported by al-Bukhari & Muslim.

36. Practising Hijama

The Prophet (peace and blessings of Allah upon him) said:

"The best medicines you may treat yourselves with are cupping and sea incense".[1]

Ibn Abbas reported:

"The Prophet (peace and blessings of Allah upon him) had a Hijama performed and paid the person who performed it for him."[2]

Anas said:

"The Prophet (peace and blessings of Allah upon him) was cupped on his head for unilateral headache while he was in a state of Ihram."[3]

Remarks:

Hijama is a therapeutic method that extracts blood from the surface of the epidermis. It is also known as cupping therapy.

---

[1] Reported by al-Bukhari & Muslim.
[2] Reported by al-Bukhari & Muslim.
[3] Reported by al-Bukhari.

37. Using Siwak

The Prophet (peace and blessings of Allah upon him) said:

"Were it not hard on my ummah, I would order them to use the toothstick at the time of every prayer."[1]

The Prophet (peace and blessings of Allah upon him) said:

"Use the siwak, for it purifies the mouth and pleases to the Lord."[2]

Miqdam ibn Shuraih narrated it from his father, who said:

"I asked 'A'isha what Allah's Apostle (peace and blessings of Allah upon him) did first when he entered his house, and she replied: 'He used tooth-stick (first of all).'"[3]

Remarks:

Siwak, also known as *miswak* or *arak stick*, is a natural toothbrush made from roots or branches.

---

[1] Reported by al-Bukhari & Muslim.
[2] Reported by Ahmad. Authenticated by al-Albani.
[3] Reported by Muslim.

38. Cutting your nails

The Prophet (peace and blessings of Allah upon him) said:

"Five are the acts quite akin to the Fitra, or five are the acts of Fitra: circumcision, shaving the pubes, cutting the nails, plucking the hair under the armpits and clipping the moustache."[1]

Remarks:

Imam an-Nawawi explains the recommended way to trim one's nails:

- Begin nail trimming with the right hand, starting with the index finger, then the middle finger, ring finger, little finger and thumb.

- Continue with the left hand, starting with the little finger.

- Start with the little toe of the right foot and finish with the little toe of the left foot.

---

[1] Reported by al-Bukhari & Muslim.

39. Getting rid of some hair

Anas reported:

"A time limit has been prescribed for us for clipping the moustache, cutting the nails, plucking the hair under the armpits, shaving the pubes, that it should not be neglected far more than forty nights."[1]

---

[1] Reported by Muslim.

40. Perfume

The Prophet (peace and blessings of Allah upon him) said:

"Women and perfume have been made dear to me, but my comfort has been provided in prayer."[1]

The Prophet (peace and blessings of Allah upon him) said:

"Whoever is offered perfume, let him not refuse it, for it is easy to carry and smells good."[2]

The Prophet (peace and blessings of Allah upon him) said:

"One of the best of your perfumes is musk."[3]

---

[1] Reported by al-Nassai. Authenticated by al-Albani.
[2] Reported by Muslim.
[3] Reported by al-Nassai. Authenticated by al-Albani.

Chapter 3: Psychology

41. Having a good opinion of Allah

Allah said:

"Say: "O My slaves who have transgressed against themselves! Despair not of the Mercy of Allah, verily Allah forgives all sins. Truly, He is Oft-Forgiving, Most Merciful."[1]

The Prophet (peace and blessings of Allah upon him) said:

"None of you should court death but only hoping good from Allah."[2]

The Prophet (peace and blessings of Allah upon him) said:

"A man used to do sinful deeds, and when death came to him, he said to his sons:'After my death, burn me and then crush me, and scatter the powder in the air, for by Allah, if Allah has control over me, He will give me such a punishment as He has never given to anyone else.' When he died, his sons did accordingly. Allah ordered the earth, saying, 'Collect

---

[1] Surah 39: The Groups, verse 53.
[2] Reported by Muslim.

what you hold of his particles.' It did so, and behold! There he was (the man) standing. Allah asked (him), 'What made you do what you did?' He replied, 'O my Lord! I was afraid of You.' So Allah forgave him."[1]

---

[1] Reported by al-Bukhari.

42. Crying

Allah said:

"And they fall on their faces weeping, and it adds to their humility."[1]

"Do you then wonder at this recital (the Qur'an)? And you laugh at it and weep not, wasting your lifetime in pastime and amusements."[2]

The Prophet (peace and blessings of Allah upon him) said:

"By Him in Whose hand is the life of Muhammad, if you could see what I see, you would have laughed little and wept much more."

They said: "What did you see, Messenger of Allah?"

He replied: *"(I saw) Paradise and Hell."*[3]

The Prophet (peace and blessings of Allah upon him) said:

"Allah will give shade to seven, on the Day when there will be no shade but His. (These seven persons are) a just ruler, a

---

[1] Surah 17: The Journey by night, verse 109.
[2] Surah 53: The Star, verses 59 to 61.
[3] Reported by Muslim.

youth who has been brought up in the worship of Allah (i.e. worships Allah sincerely from childhood), a man whose heart is attached to the mosques (i.e. to pray the compulsory prayers in the mosque in congregation), two persons who love each other only for Allah's sake and they meet and part in Allah's cause only, a man who refuses the call of a charming woman of noble birth for illicit intercourse with her and says: I am afraid of Allah, a man who gives charitable gifts so secretly that his left-hand does not know what his right hand has given (i.e. nobody knows how much he has given in charity), and a person who remembers Allah in seclusion and his eyes are then flooded with tears".[1]

---

[1] Reported by al-Bukhari & Muslim.

43. Observing the person below you

The Prophet (peace and blessings of Allah upon him) said:

"When one of you looks at one who stands at a higher level than you regarding wealth and physical structure, he should also see one who stands at a lower level than you regarding these things (in which he stands) at a higher level (as compared to him)."[1]

Remarks:

Shaykh As-Sa'di explains that if we meditated on this hadeeth, we would realise that we are privileged compared to many people. Whether in health, wealth, or even other things, most of us enjoy a very favourable situation compared to many others.

Remembering this hadeeth dispels fear, grief and anxiety. It also brings joy and satisfaction to the situation that Allah has given us.

---

[1] Reported by Muslim.

The shaykh adds that the more we pay attention to the blessings we enjoy, the more we realise that we have been spared many evils.

Finally, let's remember that these benefits can relate to the life of this world (financial situation, health, etc.) as well as that of the following (religious situation).

44. Show patience

Allah said:

"And seek help in patience and *As-Salat* (the prayer) "[1]

"And endure you patiently (O Muhammad), your patience is not but from Allah. And grieve not over them and be not distressed because of what they plot."[2]

"And bear with patience whatever befalls you."[3]

"But give glad tidings to *As-Sabirin* (the patient ones)."[4]

The Prophet (peace and blessings of Allah upon him) said:

"And whoever remains patient, Allah will make him patient. Nobody can be given a blessing better and greater than patience."[5]

The Prophet (peace and blessings of Allah upon him) said:

"Patience is a light!"[6]

---

[1] Surah 2: The Cow, verse 45.
[2] Surah 16: The Bees, verse 127.
[3] Surah 31: Luqman, verse 17.
[4] Surah 2: The Cow, verse 155.
[5] Reported by al-Bukhari.
[6] Reported by Muslim.

45. Think of the consequences of our actions

Allah said:

"Allah burdens not a person beyond his scope. He gets reward for that (good) which he has earned, and he is punished for that (evil) which he has earned."[1]

" (What is the matter with you?) When a single disaster smites you, although you smote (your enemies) with one twice as great, you say: "From where does this come to us?" Say, "It is from yourselves." And Allah has power over all things."[2]

"And whatever misfortune befalls you is because of what your hands have earned. And He pardons much."[3]

"Whatever of good reaches you is from Allah, but whatever evil befalls you is from yourself."[4]

The Prophet (peace and blessings of Allah upon him) said:

---

[1] Surah 2: The Cow, verse 286.
[2] Surah 3: Family of Imran, verse 165.
[3] Surah 42: The Consultation, verse 30.
[4] Surah 4: The Women, verse 79.

"Allah ordered (the appointed angels over you) that the good and the bad deeds be written, and He then showed (the way) how (to write). If somebody intends to do a good deed and he does not do it, then Allah will write for him a full good deed (in his account with Him). If he intends to do a good deed and did it, then Allah will write for him (in his account) with Him (its reward equal) from ten to seven hundred times to many more times: and if somebody intended to do a bad deed and he does not do it, then Allah will write a full good deed (in his account) with Him, and if he intended to do it (a bad deed) and did it, then Allah will write one bad deed (in his account)."[1]

---

[1] Reported by al-Bukhari & Muslim.

46. Not worrying about the past

The Prophet (peace and blessings of Allah upon him) said:

"Cherish that which gives you benefit (in the Hereafter) and seek help from Allah and do not lose heart, and if anything (in the form of trouble) comes to you, don't say: 'If I had not done that, it would not have happened so and so', but say: 'Allah did that what He had ordained to do and your 'if' opens the (gate) for Satan."[1]

---

[1] Reported by Muslim.

47. Not worrying about the future

The Prophet (peace and blessings of Allah upon him) said:

"Know that whatever has befallen you could not have passed you by, and whatever has passed you by could not have befallen you."[1]

---
[1] Reported by al-Tirmidhi. Authenticated by al-Albani.

48. Thinking before acting

The Prophet (peace and blessings of Allah upon him) said:

"Deliberateness is from Allah, and haste is from the shaitan."[1]

Remarks:

Taking our time and avoiding haste should not make us forget that we must hasten to do good deeds.

Allah said:

"And march forth in the way (which leads to) forgiveness from your Lord, and for Paradise as wide as are the heavens and the earth, prepared for *Al-Muttaqun* (the pious)."[2]

The Prophet (peace and blessings of Allah upon him) said: *"Be prompt in doing good deeds (before you are overtaken) by turbulence, which would be like a part of the dark night. During (that stormy period) a man would be a Muslim in the morning and an unbeliever in the evening, or he would be a believer in the evening and an unbeliever in the morning and would sell his faith for worldly goods."*[3]

---

[1] Reported by Abu Ya'la. Authenticated by al-Albani.
[2] Surah 3: Family of Imran, verse 133.
[3] Reported by Muslim.

49. Consulting Allah

Jabir - may Allah be pleased with him - reported:

"The Prophet (peace and blessings of Allah upon him) used to teach us the *Istikhara* for every matter as he used to teach us the Suras from the Holy Qur'an.(He used to say), *"If any of you intends to do something, he should offer a two rak'at prayer other than the obligatory prayer and then say: 'O Allah! I consult You, for You have all knowledge, and appeal to You to support me with Your Power and ask for Your Bounty, for You can do things while I am not, and You know while I do not; and You are the Knower of the Unseen. O Allah, if You know this matter (name your matter) is good for me both at present and in the future (or in my religion), in this life and the Hereafter, then fulfil it for me and make it easy for me, and then bestow Your Blessings on me in that matter. O Allah! If You know that this matter is not good for me in my religion, in this life and my coming Hereafter (or at present or in the future), then divert me from it and choose for me what is good wherever it may be, and make me pleased with it.'*

Then he should mention his matter (need)."[1]

---

[1] Reported by al-Bukhari.

50. Acting with constancy

The Prophet (peace and blessings of Allah upon him) said:

"The acts most pleasing to Allah are those which are done continuously, even if small."[1]

---

[1] Reported by al-Bukhari.

51. Fighting laziness

Allah said:

"And if they had intended to march out, certainly, they would have made some preparation for it, but Allah was averse to their being sent forth, so He made them lag behind, and it was said (to them), "Sit you among those who sit (at home).""[1]

"Verily, the hypocrites seek to deceive Allah, but it is He Who deceives them. And when they stand up for *As-Salat* (the prayer), they stand with laziness and to be seen of men, and they do not remember Allah but little."[2]

The Prophet (peace and blessings of Allah upon him) said:

"O Allah! I seek refuge with You from worry and grief, from incapacity and laziness, from cowardice and miserliness, from being heavily in debt and from being overpowered by (other) men."[3]

---

[1] Surah 9: The Repentance, verse 46.
[2] Surah 4: The Women, verse 142.
[3] Reported by al-Bukhari.

52. Choosing the easy way

Aisha — may Allah be pleased with her — reported:

"Whenever the Prophet (peace and blessings of Allah upon him) was given an option between two things, he used to select the easier of the two as long as it was not sinful; but if it were sinful, he would remain far from it."[1]

---

[1] Reported by al-Bukhari.

53. Fighting pride

Allah said:

"And turn not your face away from men with pride, nor walk in insolence through the earth. Verily, Allah likes not each arrogant boaster. And be moderate in your walking, and lower your voice. Verily, the harshest of all voices is the voice (braying) of the ass."[1]

The Prophet (peace and blessings of Allah upon him) said:

"He who has in his heart the weight of a mustard seed of pride shall not enter Paradise." A person (amongst his hearers) said: 'Verily a person loves that his dress should be fine, and his shoes should be fine.' The Prophet remarked:

'Verily, Allah is Graceful, and He loves Grace. Pride is disdaining the truth (out of self-conceit) and contempt for the people'".[2]

The Prophet (peace and blessings of Allah upon him) said:

"Three (are the persons) with whom Allah would neither speak, nor would He absolve them on the Day of Resurrection,

---

[1] Surah 31: Luqman, verses 18-19.
[2] Reported by Muslim.

He would not look at them, and there is grievous torment for them: the aged adulterer, the liar king and the proud destitute."[1]

The Prophet (peace and blessings of Allah upon him) said:

"Allah revealed to me that we should be humble amongst ourselves and none should show pride upon the others."[2]

---

[1] Reported by Muslim.
[2] Reported by Muslim.

54. Pushing back satanic insufflations

Allah said:

"Say: 'I seek refuge with the Lord of mankind, the King of mankind, the God of mankind, from the evil of the whisperer who withdraws, who whispers in the breasts of mankind, of jinns and men."[1]

"O you who believe! Follow not the footsteps of Satan. And whosoever follows the footsteps of Satan, then, certainly, he commands to commit indecency, disbelief and polytheism. And had it not been for the Grace of Allah and His Mercy on you, not one of you would ever have been pure from sins. But Allah purifies whom He wills, and Allah is All-Hearer, All-Knower."[2]

The Prophet (peace and blessings of Allah upon him) said: *"Satan comes to one of you and says:*

'Who created so-and-so?' till he says: 'Who has created your Lord?' So, when he inspires such a question, one should seek refuge with Allah and give up such thoughts."[3]

---

[1] Surah 114: The Mankind.
[2] Surah 24: The Light, verse 21.
[3] Reported by al-Bukhari.

Remarks:

Satanic insufflations are thoughts that cross an individual's mind. They can take root or, on the contrary, be repelled.

It should be noted that occult causes (djinns, evil eye, etc.) can also lead to psychological ills. Demons incite people to indulge their evil passions through their satanic insufflations. This can lead to anxiety disorders of various kinds. Demons also use possession to be even more effective in this type of work.

It is important to remember that these insufflations come from the devil and, above all, to repel them as soon as they arrive to prevent them from taking root.

55. Fighting your soul

Allah said:

"And by *Nafs* (Adam or a person or a soul), and Him Who perfected him in proportion; then He showed him what is wrong for him and what is right for him; indeed, he succeeds who purifies his own self. And indeed, he fails who corrupts his own self."[1]

"And I free not myself (from the blame). Verily, the (human) self is inclined to evil, except when my Lord bestows His Mercy. Verily, my Lord is Oft-Forgiving, Most Merciful."[2]

The Prophet (peace and blessings of Allah upon him) said:

"The Mujahid is the one who strives against his soul to submit it to Allah."[3]

Remarks:

To fight our soul, we need to examine it. The scholars have listed two stages in the examination of the soul:

---

[1] Surah 91: The Sun, verses 7-10.
[2] Surah 12: Joseph, verse 53.
[3] Reported by Ahmad. Authenticated by al-Albani.

- Before acting: when the soul invites us to perform an act, we must analyse it and conclude whether it contains a good or an evil.

- After having acted: examine what has been accomplished and praise Allah if it is a work of good or repent if it is an evil.

Letting go of the harness of the soul has terrible consequences for the individual's health, property and life.

56. Channeling desires

Allah said:

"But if they answer you not, then know that they only follow their lusts."[1]

"And had We willed, We would surely have elevated him in addition to that, but he clung to the earth and followed his vain desire. So his description is the description of a dog: if you drive him away, he lolls his tongue out, or if you leave him alone, he lolls his tongue out."[2]

"Those who do wrong follow their lusts without knowledge."[3]

"And obey not him whose heart We have made heedless of Our Remembrance, one who follows his lusts."[4]

"Have you (O Muhammad) seen him who has taken as his god his desire?"[5]

---

[1] Surah 28: The Stories, verse 50.
[2] Surah 7: The Heights, verse 176.
[3] Surah 30: The Romans, verse 29.
[4] Surah 18: The Cave, verse 28.
[5] Surah 25: The Criterion, verse 43.

Remarks:

Desires and impulses must be satisfied within the framework of the Creator's Legislation (for example, sexual desire satisfied within marriage).

The soul feeds on passions. Passions are actions that serve to satisfy our desires and urges.

Some passions are necessary and praiseworthy, while others are harmful. So, we need to distinguish between good and evil passions.

Indulging harmful passions leads to physical and psychological suffering: physical and mental fatigue, guilt, frustration due to the ephemeral nature of pleasure, and false hopes.

Performing good deeds and abandoning sins calms the passions.

57. Fighting envy

Allah said:

"And to everyone, We have appointed heirs of that left by parents and relatives. To those also with whom you have made a pledge, give them their due portion. Truly, Allah is Ever a Witness over all things."[1]

The Prophet (peace and blessings of Allah upon him) said:"No, bondsman (truly) believes till he likes for his brother, whatever he likes for himself."[2]

The Prophet (peace and blessings of Allah upon him) said:

"Not to wish to be the like of except two men: A man whom Allah has taught the Qur'an and he recites it during the hours of the night and the hours of the day, and his neighbor listens to him and says, 'I wish I had been given what has been given to so-and-so, so that I might do what he does; and a man whom Allah has given wealth and he spends it on what is just and right, after that another man may say, 'I wish I had been given what so-and-so has been given, for then I would do what he does.'"[3]

---
[1] Surah 4: The Women, verse 32.
[2] Reported by al-Bukhari & Muslim.
[3] Reported by al-Bukhari.

58. Controlling anger

Allah said:

"Those who spend in prosperity and adversity, repress anger, and pardon men; verily, Allah loves the good-doers."[1]

The Prophet (peace and blessings of Allah upon him) said:

"The strong is not the one who overcomes the people by his strength, but the strong is the one who controls himself in anger."[2]

Sulayman ibn Surad reported that two persons abused each other in the presence of Allah's Apostle (peace and blessings of Allah upon him), and the eyes of one of them became red as embers, and the veins of his neck were swollen. Thereupon Allah's Messenger (peace and blessings of Allah upon him) said:

"I know of a wording, if he were to utter that, his fit of rage (would be no more and that wording is): "I seek refuge with Allah from Satan the accursed.""[3]

Abu Hurayra reported:

---

[1] Surah 3: Family of Imran, verse 134.
[2] Reported by al-Bukhari & Muslim.
[3] Reported by Muslim.

"A man said to the Prophet (peace and blessings of Allah upon him):

"Advise me!"

The Prophet (peace and blessings of Allah upon him) said:

"Do not become angry and furious."

The man asked (the same) again and again, and the Prophet (peace and blessings of Allah upon him) said in each case: *"Do not become angry and furious."*[1]

---

[1] Reported by al-Bukhari.

59. Moderate laughter

The Prophet (peace and blessings of Allah upon him) said:

"For laughing a lot deadens the heart." [1]

The Prophet (peace and blessings of Allah upon him) said:

"A servant does not fully believe until he abandons lying even in jest and avoids arguing, even when he is sincere." [2]

Remarks:

Imam An-Nawawi explained moderation in laughter and joking by saying:"The scholars have said that the forbidden joke is that which is excessive and constant, for it causes [excessive] laughter, hardening of the heart, neglect of the invocation of Allah the Most High and of reflection on important matters of religion [..]. What is exempt from this is permitted.".

---

[1] Reported by Ibn Majah. Authenticated by al-Albani.
[2] Reported by Ahmad. Authenticated by al-Albani.

60. Avoiding controversy

The Prophet (peace and blessings of Allah upon him) said:

"I guarantee a house in the surroundings of Paradise for a man who avoids quarrelling even if he were in the right, a house in the middle of Paradise for a man who avoids lying even if he were joking, and a house in the upper part of Paradise for a man who made his character good."[1]

Remarks:

Shaykh Al-'Uthaymeen specifies, however, that one should not abandon a controversy whose aim is the victory of truth. But this is an exception.

---

[1] Reported by Abu Dawud. Authenticated by al-Albani.

Chapter 4: Family & Relationships

61. Smile

The Prophet (peace and blessings of Allah upon him) said:

"Smiling at your brother is a charity, commanding good and forbidding evil is a charity, guiding a man in a land of misguidance is a charity, assisting a man with poor sight is a charity, removing stones and thorns from the path is a charity, and pouring from your bucket into your brother's is a charity."[1]

The Prophet (peace and blessings of Allah upon him) said:

"Don't consider anything insignificant out of good things, even if it is that you meet your brother with a cheerful countenance."[2]

---

[1] Reported by Ibn Hibban. Authenticated by al-Albani.
[2] Reported by Muslim.

62. Offering gifts

The Prophet (peace and blessings of Allah upon him) said:

"Give gifts to each other, and you will love each other."[1]

'Aisha — may Allah be pleased with her — reported:

"Allah's Messenger (peace and blessings of Allah upon him) used to accept gifts and used to give something in return."[2]

Remarks:

The Prophet (peace and blessings of Allah upon him) used to accept gifts and offer something of equal or greater value in return.

---

[1] Reported by al-Bukhari. (in *Al-Adab Al-Moufrad*). Authenticated by al-Albani.
[2] Reported by al-Bukhari.

63. Visiting the sick

The Prophet (peace and blessings of Allah upon him) said:

"The rights of a Muslim on the Muslims are five: to respond to the salaam, to visit the sick, to follow the funeral processions, to accept an invitation, and to reply to those who sneeze."[1]

The Prophet (peace and blessings of Allah upon him) said:

"Feed the hungry, visit the sick, and set free the captives."[2]

The Prophet (peace and blessings of Allah upon him) said:

"He who visits a sick person enters into the mercy of Allah until he sits down. When he sits, he is submerged in it."[3]

The Prophet (peace and blessings of Allah upon him), when visiting a patient, used to say:

"No harm will befall you! May Allah cure you!"[4]

---

[1] Reported by al-Bukhari & Muslim.
[2] Reported by al-Bukhari.
[3] Reported by Ahmad. Authenticated by al-Albani.
[4] Reported by al-Bukhari.

Anas Ibn Malik — may Allah be pleased with him — reported: "A young Jewish boy used to serve the Prophet (peace and blessings of Allah upon him), and he became sick. So the Prophet (peace and blessings of Allah upon him) visited him. He sat near his head and asked the boy to embrace Islam. The boy looked at his father, who told him to obey Abul-Qasim (The Prophet), and the boy embraced Islam. The Prophet (peace and blessings of Allah upon him) came out saying: *"Praises be to Allah Who saved the boy from the Hell-fire."*[1]

---

[1] Reported by al-Bukhari.

64. Reply to invitation

The Prophet (peace and blessings of Allah upon him) said:

"The worst food is that of a wedding banquet to which only the rich are invited while the poor are not invited. And he who refuses an invitation (to a banquet) disobeys Allah and His Apostle (peace and blessings of Allah upon him)."[1]

The Prophet (peace and blessings of Allah upon him) said:

"The rights of a Muslim on the Muslims are five: to respond to the salaam, to visit the sick, to follow the funeral processions, to accept an invitation, and to reply to those who sneeze."[2]

Remarks:

Some scholars have considered it obligatory to respond to the invitation if no conditions are preventing it. However, there are other opinions which consider this to be recommended.

---

[1] Reported by al-Bukhari & Muslim.
[2] Reported by al-Bukhari & Muslim.

65. Hiding other people's faults

The Prophet (peace and blessings of Allah upon him) said:

"He who conceals (the faults) of a Muslim, Allah would conceal his faults in the world and the Hereafter."[1] The Prophet (peace and blessings of Allah upon him) said:

"The servant (who conceals) the faults of others in this world, Allah would conceal his faults on the Day of Resurrection."[2]

The Prophet (peace and blessings of Allah upon him) said:

"He who learns a sin from his brother and conceals it, Allah will conceal his sins on the Day of Resurrection."[3]

Remarks:

Shaykh Al-'Uthaymeen explained that Allah will assign to the person who persists in looking for faults in others a person who will do the same with him and spread them.

---
[1] Reported by Muslim.
[2] Reported by Muslim.
[3] Reported by al-Tabarani. Authenticated by al-Albani.

These people like to find fault in people because they want to tell others about them. Punishment can also consist of revealing the most secret sins in one way or another.

66. Giving advice

Allah said:

"Go, both of you, to Pharaoh, verily, he has transgressed. And speak to him mildly, perhaps he may accept admonition or fear Allah."[1]

"So remind them, you are only a one who reminds. You are not a dictator over them."[2]

The Prophet (peace and blessings of Allah upon him) said:

"Religion consists of sincere conduct. Religion consists of sincere conduct. Religion consists of sincere conduct."

The people asked: to whom should it be directed, Messenger of Allah? He replied:

"To Allah, his book, his Apostle, the leaders (public authorities) of the believers and all the believers, and the leaders (public authorities) of Muslims and the Muslims in general".[3]

---

[1] Surah 20: Ta-Ha, verses 43-44.
[2] Surah 88: The Overwhelming : verse 21.
[3] Reported by Abu Dawud. Authenticated by al-Albani.

67. Responding to evil with good

Allah said:

"The good deed and the evil deed cannot be equal. Repel (the evil) with one which is better, then verily! he, between whom and you there was enmity, (will become) as though he was a close friend."[1]

---

[1] Surah 41: Explained in detail, verse 34.

68. No spying

"O you who believe! Avoid much suspicions, indeed some suspicions are sins. And spy not, neither backbite one another."[1] The Prophet (peace and blessings of Allah upon him) ascended the Minbar and called out with a raised voice: 'O you who accepted Islam with his tongue, while faith has not reached his heart! Do not harm the Muslims, nor revile them, nor spy on them to expose their secrets. For indeed whoever tries to expose his Muslim brother's secrets, Allah exposes his secrets wide open, even if he were in the depth of his house.'"[2]

Remarks:

Shaykh Al-'Uthaymeen explains that spying consists of trying to discover another person's secrets and private life by various means (e.g., recording, filming).

He adds that it is a forbidden practice, as it harms the person being spied upon and leads to hatred and hostility.

---

[1] Surah 49: The Dwellings, verse 12.
[2] Reported by al-Tirmidhi. Authenticated by al-Albani.

69. Telling the truth

Allah said:

"O you who believe! Be afraid of Allah, and be with those who are true (in words and deeds)."[1]

"It is only those who believe not in the *Ayat* (proofs, evidences, verses, etc.) of Allah, who fabricate falsehood, and it is they who are liars."[2]

"Then, who does more wrong than one who utters a lie against Allah and denies the truth when it comes to him? Is there not in Hell an abode for the disbelievers?"[3]

The Prophet (peace and blessings of Allah upon him) said:

"The signs of a hypocrite are three: whenever he speaks, he tells a lie. Whenever he promises, he always breaks it (his promise). If you trust him, he proves to be dishonest. (If you keep something as a trust with him, he will not return it.)"[4]

The Prophet (peace and blessings of Allah upon him) said:

---

[1] Surah 9: The Repentance, verse 119.
[2] Surah 16: The Bees, verse 105.
[3] Surah 39: The Groups, verse 32.
[4] Reported by al-Bukhari & Muslim.

"Truthfulness leads to righteousness, and righteousness leads to Paradise. And a man keeps on telling the truth until he becomes a truthful person. Falsehood leads to Al-Fajur (i.e. wickedness, evil-doing), and Al-Fajur (wickedness) leads to the (Hell) Fire, and a man may keep on telling lies till he is written before Allah, a liar." [1]

The Prophet (peace and blessings of Allah upon him) said:

"Whoever lies about me intentionally will surely take his place in the (Hell) Fire." [2]

---

[1] Reported by al-Bukhari & Muslim.
[2] Reported by Muslim.

70. Behaving well with parents

Allah said:

"Worship Allah and join none with Him in worship, and do good to parents."[1]

"And We have enjoined on man to be dutiful and kind to his parents. His mother bears him with hardship, and she brings him forth with hardship, and the bearing of him, and the weaning of him is thirty months, till when he attains full strength and reaches forty years, he says: "My Lord! Grant me the power and ability to be grateful for Your Favour, which You have bestowed upon me and my parents, and that I may do righteous deeds, such as please You, and make my offspring good. Truly, I have turned to You in repentance, and truly, I am one of the Muslims.""[2]

"And We have enjoined on man to his parents. His mother bore him in weakness and hardship upon weakness and hardship, and his weaning is in two years give thanks to Me and to your parents; unto Me is the final destination. But if they (both) strive with you to make you

---
[1] Surah 4: The Women, verse 36.
[2] Surah 46: The Curved Sand-Hills, verse 15.

join in worship with Me others that of which you have no knowledge, then obey them not, but behave with them in the world kindly, and follow the path of him who turns to Me in repentance and obedience. Then to Me will be your return, and I shall tell you what you used to do."[1]

"And your Lord has decreed that you worship none but Him. And that you be dutiful to your parents. If one or both of them attain old age in your life, say not to them a word of disrespect, nor shout at them, but address them in terms of honour. And lower unto them the wing of submission and humility through mercy, and say: "My Lord! Bestow on them Your Mercy as they did bring me up when I was small.""[2]

A man came to Allah's Messenger (peace and blessings of Allah upon him) and said, "O Allah's Messenger! Who is more entitled to be treated with the best companionship by me?"

The Prophet (peace and blessings of Allah upon him) said, *"Your mother."*

The man said. "Who is next?"

The Prophet said, *"Your mother."*

The man further said, "Who is next?"

---

[1] Surah 31: Luqman, verses 14-15.
[2] Surah 17: The Journey by night, verses 23-24.

The Prophet (peace and blessings of Allah upon him) said, *"Your mother."*

The man asked for the fourth time, "Who is next?"

The Prophet (peace and blessings of Allah upon him) said, *"Your father."*[1]

Ibn Mas'ud – may Allah be pleased with him – reported:

"I asked the Prophet (peace and blessings of Allah upon him) 'Which deed is loved most by Allah?"

He replied, *'To offer prayers at their early (very first) stated times.'* Abdullah asked, "What is the next (in goodness)?"

The Prophet (peace and blessings of Allah upon him) said, *"To be good and dutiful to one's parents,"*

'Abdullah asked, "What is the next (in goodness)?"

The Prophet (peace and blessings of Allah upon him) said, *"To participate in Jihad for Allah's Cause."*[2]

Remarks:

Shaykh Al-'Uthaymeen explains that parents have rights over their children because of what they endure for them. This is particularly true for the mother, who suffers a great deal before, during and after the birth of her children. The father also has a vital role to play. In fact, he does everything possible to ensure that his children lack nothing, no matter

---

[1] Reported by al-Bukhari & Muslim.
[2] Reported by al-Bukhari & Muslim.

what he has to endure. The shaykh adds that, whatever our actions, we will never be able to compensate for all their rights.

It is therefore obligatory for us to make a habit of behaving well towards our parents and being devoted to them.

71. Behaving well as husband and wife

Allah said:

"They are *Libas* (body cover) for you, and you are the same for them "[1]

The Prophet (peace and blessings of Allah upon him) said:

"A believer must not hate a believing woman; if he dislikes one of her characteristics, he will be pleased with another."[2]

The Prophet (peace and blessings of Allah upon him) said:

"The most complete of the believers in faith is the one with the best character. And the best of you are those who are best to your women."[3]

The Prophet (peace and blessings of Allah upon him) said:

---

[1] Surah 2 : The Cow, verse 187.
[2] Reported by Muslim.
[3] Reported by al-Tirmidhi. Authenticated by al-Albani.

"If I were to order anyone to prostrate to anyone, then I would order the wife to prostrate to her husband."[1]

The Prophet (peace and blessings of Allah upon him) said:

"If the woman performs her five (prayers), fasts her month (Ramadan), preserves her sex and obeys her husband, then she will be told: "Enter Paradise through whichever of its gates you wish.""[2]

---

[1] Reported by al-Tirmidhi. Authenticated by al-Albani.
[2] Reported by Ahmad. Authenticated by Al-Albani.

72. Behaving well with children

The Prophet (peace and blessings of Allah upon him) said:

"Be afraid of Allah, and be just to your children."[1]

A bedouin came to the Prophet (peace and blessings of Allah upon him) and said, "You (people) kiss the boys! We don't kiss them."

The Prophet (peace and blessings of Allah upon him) said, *"I cannot put mercy in your heart after Allah has taken it away from it."*[2]

Remarks:

Shaykh Ferkous explains that Islam encourages exemplary behaviour and patience with children without being harsh or severe. By being gentle with children and giving them the affection they need, they can only be gentle and kind in turn.

Complimenting children and recognising their good deeds are also part of being gentle with them. It's also

---

[1] Reported by al-Bukhari.
[2] Reported by Muslim.

important to instil good habits (food, clothing, hygiene, etc.) in them from an early age.

All these principles apply equally to all the children in the household. There should be no difference between them in terms of affection, love, material needs, education and protection.

73. Behaving well with neighbours

Allah said:

"Worship Allah and join none with Him in worship, and do good to parents, kinsfolk, orphans, the poor, the neighbour who is near of kin, the neighbour who is a stranger, the companion by your side, the wayfarer, and those (slaves) whom your right hands possess. Verily, Allah does not like such as are proud and boastful."[1]

The Prophet (peace and blessings of Allah upon him) said:

"Gabriel continued to recommend that I treat the neighbours kindly and politely, so much so that I thought he would order me to make them my heirs."[2]

The Prophet (peace and blessings of Allah upon him) said:

"Anybody who believes in Allah and the Last Day should serve his neighbour generously."[3]

---

[1] Surah 4: The Women, verse 36.
[2] Reported by Muslim.
[3] Reported by al-Bukhari & Muslim.

The Prophet (peace and blessings of Allah upon him) said:

"By Allah, he is not a believer! By Allah, he is not a believer! By Allah, he is not a believer."

It was asked, "Who is that, O Messenger of Allah?"

He said, *"One whose neighbour does not feel safe from his evil"*.[1]

Remarks:

In one of his sermons, Shaykh Abderrazaq Al-Badr explains that a neighbour is someone whose home is close by and whom we are used to meeting. As the quoted texts show, he has rights towards us.

Shaykh Abderrazzaq Al-Badr adds that sometimes vanity, pride and arrogance prevent us from behaving well towards our neighbour. On the other hand, modesty and faith prevent us from neglecting our neighbour's rights.

Finally, we learn that excellent neighbourly behaviour can be summed up in two main points:

- Showing respect for your neighbour
- Spare him from our evil.

---

[1] Reported by al-Bukhari.

74. Minding our own business

The Prophet (peace and blessings of Allah upon him) said:

"Indeed, among the excellence of a person's Islam is that he leaves what does not concern him."[1]

Remarks:

Shaykh Al-'Uthaymeen has explained this hadeeth. He indicates that this text concerns both our religion and our life in this world.

He adds that it is inappropriate to be interested in people's affairs, mainly by asking indiscreet questions. This is part of the beautiful Islam, and rest is therein. Indeed, taking an interest in other people's affairs is accompanied by significant fatigue and a massive waste of time. We, therefore, miss out on things that are profitable for us. It is, thus, preferable to take care of what concerns us to avoid these inconveniences.

The shaykh advises us to concentrate on what is useful to us and to neglect what is not. He observes that many people torment their hearts and thoughts with the affairs

---

[1] Reported by al-Tirmidhi. Authenticated by al-Albani.

of others. As a result, they lose strength that could help them correct their own situation.

75. Ask permission before entering

Allah said:

"O you who believe! Enter not houses other than your own until you have asked permission and greeted those in them that are better for you so that you may remember. And if you find no one therein, still, enter not until permission has been given. And if you are asked to go back, go back, for it is purer for you, and Allah is All-Knower of what you do."[1]

The Prophet (peace and blessings of Allah upon him) said:

"When one of you asks permission three times, and it is not granted to him, he should go away."[2]

---
[1] Surah 24: The Light, verses 27-28.
[2] Reported by al-Bukhari & Muslim.

76. Lower your gaze

Allah said:

"Tell the believing men to lower their gaze and protect their private parts. That is purer for them. Verily, Allah is All-Aware of what they do. And tell the believing women to lower their gaze, and protect their private parts and not to show off their adornment except only that which is apparent."[1]

"Verily! The hearing, the sight, and the heart of each of those you will be questioned (by Allah). "[2]

The Prophet (peace and blessings of Allah upon him) said:

"Allah has written for the son of Adam his inevitable share of adultery whether he is aware of it or not: The adultery of the eye is the looking (at something which is sinful to look at)."[3]

---

[1] Surah 24: The Light, verses 30-31.
[2] Surah 17: The Journey by night, verse 36.
[3] Reported by al-Bukhari & Muslim.

77. Avoid flattery

The Prophet (peace and blessings of Allah upon him) heard someone praising another and exaggerating his praise. The Prophet (peace and blessings of Allah upon him) said *"You have ruined the man's back (by praising him so much)."*[1]

A man praised another man in front of the Prophet (peace and blessings of Allah upon him). The Prophet (peace and blessings of Allah upon him) said to him: *"Woe to you, you have cut off your companion's neck, you have cut off your companion's neck,"* repeating it several times and then added:

"Whoever amongst you has to praise his brother should say, 'I think that he is so and so, and Allah knows exactly the truth, and I do not confirm anybody's good conduct before Allah, but I think him so and so,' if he knows what he says about him."[2]

A person began to praise 'Uthman and Miqdad sat upon his knee; and he was a bulky person and began to throw pebbles upon his (flatterer's) face. Thereupon 'Uthman said:

---

[1] Reported by al-Bukhari & Muslim.
[2] Reported by al-Bukhari & Muslim.

What is the matter with you? And he said: Verily, Allah's Messenger (peace and blessings of Allah upon him) said:

"When you see those who shower (undue) praise (upon others), throw dust upon their faces."[1]

Remarks:

Some commentators think that exaggeration in praising another is a path to falsehood.

They state, however, that praising a man for his good deeds so that he is taken as a model is not considered flattery.

---

[1] Reported by Muslim.

78. Avoid using foul language

Allah said:

"Allah does not like that the evil should be uttered in public except by him who has been wronged."[1]

The Prophet (peace and blessings of Allah upon him) said:

"Indecency and vulgarity are not part of Islam in any way, and the best of people in terms of their Islam are those who have the best character."[2]

The Prophet (peace and blessings of Allah upon him) said:

"Abusing a Muslim is Fusuq (an evil doing), and killing him is Kufr (disbelief)."[3]

The Prophet (peace and blessings of Allah upon him) said:

"When two persons indulge in hurling (abuses) upon one another, it would be the first one who would be the sinner so long as the oppressed does not transgress the limits."[4]

---
[1] Surah 4: The Women, verse 148.
[2] Reported by Ahmad. Authenticated by al-Albani.
[3] Reported by al-Bukhari & Muslim.
[4] Reported by Muslim.

The Prophet (peace and blessings of Allah upon him) said:

"*The believer does not insult the honour of others, nor curse, nor commit Fahishah, nor is he foul.*"[1]

---

[1] Reported by al-Tirmidhi. Authenticated by al-Albani.

79. Being grateful

Allah said:

"Give thanks to Me and to your parents."[1]

The Prophet (peace and blessings of Allah upon him) said:

"Speaking of Allah's blessings is an act of gratitude, whereas neglecting to mention them is disbelief. Whoever does not thank the little will not thank the much. Whoever does not thank people does not thank Allah. Unity is a blessing, and division is a torment."[2]

The Prophet (peace and blessings of Allah upon him) said:

"Whoever some good was done to him, and he says: 'May Allah reward you in goodness.' then he has done the most that he can of praise."[3]

---

[1] Surah 31: Luqman, verse 14.
[2] Reported by al-Bayhaqi. Authenticated by al-Albani.
[3] Reported by al-Tirmidhi. Authenticated by al-Albani.

80. Saluting others

Allah said: "But when you enter the houses, greet one another with a greeting from Allah blessed and good."[1]

"When you are greeted with a greeting, greet in return with what is better than it, or (at least) return it equally. Certainly, Allah is Ever a Careful Accountant of all things."[2]

The Prophet (peace and blessings of Allah upon him) said:

"Six are the rights of a Muslim over another Muslim: When you meet him, offer him greetings; when he invites you to a feast, accept it; when he seeks your council, give him, and when he sneezes and says: "All praise is due to Allah, "you say Yarhamuk Allah (may Allah show mercy to you), and when he fails ill visit him; and when he dies follow his bier."[3]

A man asked the Prophet, "What Islamic traits are the best?"

The Prophet (peace and blessings of Allah upon him) said:

---

[1] Surah 24: The Light, verse 61.
[2] Surah 4: The Women, verse 86.
[3] Reported by Muslim.

"Feed the people, and greet those you know and those you do not know."[1]

---
[1] Reported by al-Bukhari & Muslim.

Chapter 5: Finance

81. Getting up early

Sakhr Al-Ghamidi — may Allah be pleased with him — reported: "The Prophet (peace and blessings of Allah upon him) said:

"O Allah, bless my people in their early mornings."

When he sent out a detachment or an army, he sent them at the beginning of the day. Sakhr was a merchant, and he would send off his merchandise at the beginning of the day. He became rich and had much wealth.[1]

It is reported that Ibn 'Abbas saw one of his children sleeping in the early morning and said to him:

"Are you sleeping at the time when subsistence is being distributed?".

---

[1] Reported by Abu Dawud. Authenticated by al-Albani.

82. Working

The Prophet (peace and blessings of Allah upon him) said:

"For one of you to go out early to gather firewood and carry it on his back so that he can give charity from it and be free of need from the people is better for him than to ask a man who may give that to him or refuse. Indeed the upper hand (giving) is more virtuous than the lower hand (receiving), and begin with (those who are) your dependants."[1]

The Prophet (peace and blessings of Allah upon him) said:

"Nobody has ever eaten a better meal than that which one has earned by working with one's own hands. The Prophet (peace be upon him) of Allah, David, used to eat from the earnings of his manual labour."[2]

---

[1] Reported by al-Tirmidhi. Authenticated by al-Albani.
[2] Reported by al-Bukhari.

83. Doing business

Allah said:

"Then when the (Jumu'ah) Salat (prayer) is finished, you may disperse through the land and seek the Bounty of Allah."[1]

"Those who eat usury will not stand except like the standing of a person beaten by Satan, leading him to insanity. That is because they say: "Trading is only like usury," whereas Allah has permitted trading and forbidden usury. So whosoever receives an admonition from his Lord and stops eating usury shall not be punished for the past; his case is for Allah; but whoever returns, such are the dwellers of the Fire – they will abide therein."[2]

The Prophet (peace and blessings of Allah upon him) said:

"The seller and the buyer have the right to keep or return goods as long as they have not parted or till they part; and if both the parties spoke the truth and described the defects and qualities (of the goods), then they would be blessed in their

---

[1] Surah 62: Friday, verse 10.
[2] Surah 2: The Cow, verse 275.

transaction, and if they told lies or hid something, then the blessings of their transaction would be lost."[1]

The Prophet (peace and blessings of Allah upon him) said:

"May Allah's mercy be on him, who is lenient in buying, selling, and demanding back his money."[2]

---

[1] Reported by al-Bukhari & Muslim.
[2] Reported by al-Bukhari.

84. Getting married

Allah said:

"And marry those among you who are single and (also marry) the pious of your (male) slaves and maid-servants (female slaves). If they are poor, Allah will enrich them out of His Bounty. And Allah is All-Sufficent for His creatures' needs, All-Knowing."[1]

The Prophet (peace and blessings of Allah upon him) said:

"There are three for whom it is a right upon Allah to help him: The Mujahid in the cause of Allah, the Mukatab who intends to fulfil (the Kitabah), and the one getting married who intends chastity."[2]

It is reported that Abu Bakr said :

"Obey Allah by marrying, and He will grant you the wealth He has promised you."

It is reported that 'Umar Ibn Al-Khattab said :

---

[1] Surah 24: The Light, verse 32.
[2] Reported by al-Tirmidhi. Authenticated by al-Albani.

"It is astonishing that men did not seek wealth in marriage when Allah said: "If they are poor, Allah will enrich them out of His Bounty."

It is reported that Ibn Mas'ud said: "Seek wealth in marriage."

85. Spending on good

Allah said:

"Say: "Truly, my Lord enlarges the provision for whom He wills of His slaves, and (also) restricts (it) for him, and whatsoever you spend of anything, He will replace it. And He is the Best of providers.""[1]

The Prophet (peace and blessings of Allah upon him) said:

"Allah said

'Spend (O man), and I shall spend on you."[2]

The Prophet (peace and blessings of Allah upon him) said:

"Every day, two angels come down from Heaven, and one of them says,'O Allah! Compensate every person who spends in Your Cause,'and the other (angel) says,'O Allah! Destroy every miser.'"[3]

---

[1] Surah 34: Sheba, verse 39.
[2] Reported by al-Bukhari & Muslim.
[3] Reported by al-Bukhari & Muslim.

86. Spending on students of religious science

Anas Ibn Malik reported:

"There were two brothers during the time of the Messenger of Allah (peace and blessings of Allah upon him). One of them used to come to the prophet (peace and blessings of Allah upon him), and the other had some business. The businessman among them complained to the Prophet (peace and blessings of Allah upon him) about his brother, so he said:

'Perhaps you are provided for because of him.'"[1]

---

[1] Reported by al-Tirmidhi. Authenticated by al-Albani.

87. Preserving family ties

The Prophet (peace and blessings of Allah upon him) said:

"Whoever desires an expansion in his sustenance and age should keep good relations with his Kith and kin."[1]

Remarks:

Abderrazak Mahri, author of the book "The causes of the increase in subsistence", explains that maintaining family ties consists in particular of:

- visiting relatives
- helping them financially if necessary
- protecting them
- being kind to them
- invoking for them.

---

[1] Reported by al-Bukhari & Muslim.

88. Helping the weakest

The Prophet (peace and blessings of Allah upon him) said:

"You gain no victory or livelihood except through (the blessings and invocations of) the poor amongst you."[1]

Remarks:

Scholars consider the weakest of the weak to be women, children, the elderly, the poor, the sick, and foreigners passing through. Helping them must, therefore, be adapted to each case.

---

[1] Reported by al-Bukhari.

89. Making the afterlife your main concern main

Allah said:

"And enjoin the prayer on your family, and be patient in offering them. We ask not of you a provision; We provide for you. And the good end is for the pious."[1]

The Prophet (peace and blessings of Allah upon him) said:

"Whoever makes the Hereafter his goal, Allah makes his heart rich, organises his affairs, and the world comes to him whether it wants to or not. And whoever makes the world his goal, Allah puts his poverty right before his eyes and disorganises his affairs, and the world does not come to him except what has been decreed for him."[2]

---

[1] Surah 20: Ta-Ha, verse 132.
[2] Reported by al-Tirmidhi. Classified as Hasan by al-Albani.

90. Alternate between Hajj and 'Umrah

The Prophet (peace and blessings of Allah upon him) said:

"Alternate between Hajj and Umrah; for those two remove poverty and sins just as the bellows removes filth from iron, gold, and silver, and there is no reward for Al-Hajj Al-Mabrur except for Paradise."[1]

Remarks:

Abderrazak Mahri explains that these two forms of worship can eliminate poverty in man in 2 ways:

- He can become well-off
- He can see his subsistence blessed. In other words, what he has fills his heart with wealth and contentment. So even if outwardly it may seem that he is living a modest life, he is satisfied with it.

---

[1] Reported by al-Tirmidhi. Authenticated by al-Albani.

91. Doing good

The Prophet (peace and blessings of Allah upon him) said:

"When a non-believer does good, he is made to taste Its reward in this world. And so far as the believer is concerned, Allah stores (the reward) of his virtues for the Hereafter and provides him sustenance in accordance with his obedience to Him."[1]

---
[1] Reported by Muslim.

92. Hiding your plans

The Prophet (peace and blessings of Allah upon him) said:

"Seek assistance in the fulfilment of your needs by keeping them secret, for every possessor of blessings is envied."[1]

Remarks:

Based on this hadeeth, some scholars explain that it is preferable not to reveal one's plans. This is to protect oneself from the jealousy of envious people.

Shaykh Al-'Uthyamin, on the other hand, explains that telling others about one's plans can help gain their support. He adds, however, that we live in an age where jealousy is prevalent and that it is sometimes better to refrain from divulging information about one's plans.

He concludes by saying that it's up to us to see where our interests lie. If we want to, we can talk about it, and if we don't want to, we don't talk about it.

---

[1] Reported by al-Tabarani. Authenticated by al-Albani.

93. Only consume what is lawful

Allah said:

" O you who believe! Be afraid of Allah and give up what remains from usury if you are believers. If you do not do it, then take notice of war from Allah and His Messenger, but if you repent, you shall have your capital sums. Deal not unjustly, and you shall not be dealt with unjustly."[1]

The Prophet (peace and blessings of Allah upon him) said:

"Verily, the Holy Spirit (Gabriel) has breathed into my mind that no soul shall die until it has completed its term of life and its sustenance. So fear Allah and be graceful in pursuit. Do not let the delay of sustenance lead you to seek it through disobedience to Allah, for surely what is with Allah can only be attained by obeying Him."[2]

---

[1] Surah 2: The Cow, verses 278-279.
[2] Reported by Abu Nuaym. Authenticated by al-Albani.

94. Keeping to the right path

Allah said:

"If they (non-Muslims) had believed in Allah and went on the Right Way, We should indeed have bestowed on them water (rain) in abundance."[1]

---

[1] Surah 72: The Jinn, verse 16.

95. Being grateful to Allah

Allah said:

"If you give thanks, I will give you more (of My Blessings), but if you are thankless, verily! My Punishment is indeed severe."[1]

"Indeed there was for Sheba a sign in their dwelling place, – two gardens on the right hand and on the left "Eat of the provision of your Lord, and be grateful to Him, a fair land and an Oft-Forgiving Lord. But they turned away, so We sent against them *Sail Al-'Arim* (flood released from the dam), and We converted their two gardens into gardens producing bitter bad fruit, and tamarisks, and some few lote-trees."[2]

---

[1] Surah 14: Abraham, verse 7.
[2] Surah 34: Sheba, verses 15-16.

96. Asking Allah for forgiveness

Allah said: "I said (to them): 'Ask forgiveness from your Lord; Verily, He is Oft-Forgiving. He will send rain to you in abundance'"[1]

"Seek the forgiveness of your Lord, and turn to Him in repentance, that He may grant you good enjoyment, for a term appointed, and bestow His abounding Grace to every owner of grace. But if you turn away, then I fear for you the torment of a Great Day."[2]

"And O my people! Ask for forgiveness from your Lord and then repent to Him; He will send you abundant rain and add strength to your strength, so do not turn away like Mujrimun (criminals and disbelievers in the Oneness of Allah).[3]

---

[1] Surah 71: Noah, verses 10-12.
[2] Surah 11: Hud, verse 3.
[3] Surah 11: Hud, verse 52.

97. Fearing Allah

Allah said:

"And if the people of the towns had believed and had the piety, certainly, We should have opened blessings from the heaven and the earth for them, but they belied. So We took them for what they used to earn."[1]

---
[1] Surah 7: The Heights, verse 96.

98. Applying what was revealed

Allah said:

"And if only they had acted according to the Torah, the Gospel, and what has been sent down to them from their Lord (the *Qur'an*), they would surely have gotten provision from above them and underneath their feet. There are from among them people who are on the right course, but many of them do evil deeds."[1]

The Prophet (peace and blessings of Allah upon him) said:

"Carrying out a Hadd punishment in a land is better for its people than if it were to rain for forty nights."[2]

---

[1] Surah 5: The Table spread with food, verse 66.
[2] Reported by al-Nasai. Authenticated by al-Albani.

99. Claiming protection against poverty

The Prophet (peace and blessings of Allah upon him) said:

"And I seek refuge with You from the affliction of poverty." [1]

---

[1] Reported by al-Bukhari.

100. Trusting in Allah

Allah said:

"And whosoever trusts Allah, then He will suffice him."[1]

The Prophet (peace and blessings of Allah upon him) said:

"If you were to rely upon Allah with the required reliance, then He would provide for you just as a bird is provided for; it goes out in the morning empty and returns full."[2]

---

[1] Surah 65: The Divorce, verse 3.
[2] Reported by al-Tirmidhi. Authenticated by al-Albani.

Conclusion

Thank you for reading this book to the end. It will help you to improve your life, even with just one of these principles.

Praise be to Allah, Lord of the Worlds, and may the Prayer and Peace of Allah be upon our Prophet Muhammad, his family and Companions.

www.ingramcontent.com/pod-product-compliance
Lightning Source LLC
Chambersburg PA
CBHW030522080526
44586CB00011B/298